NECESSARY

for

JESUS

70 Prophecies
70 Rewards

Stephen R. Kirkendall
the two-legged wolf hunter

ISBN 978-1-0980-0675-4 (paperback)
ISBN 978-1-0980-0676-1 (digital)

Christian Faith Publishing, Inc.
832 Park Avenue
Meadville, PA 16335
www.christianfaithpublishing.com

Printed in the United States of America

Dedication

With special thanks to Kathleen M Kirkendall; Rachelle; Heather; Eva; Taylor; Paige; Amy; Colton; Jaylynn; Rob; Jason; Michael Jr.; Jordan and all the rest of my extended family starting with Jenny and King's Church who adopted me as a grandpa!

INTRODUCTION

It **was necessary** for God's design that Jesus, the Messiah, be born to die for our sins. Having fulfilled at least seventy prophecies that were written down from 500 to 1,400 years before He was born, Jesus has to be who God's Word says He is. Jesus has only asked us to help others. James 2:8 says, "If you really fulfill the royal law according to the Scripture, 'You shall love your neighbor as yourself,' you do well." To encourage us, he gave us at least seventy different rewards for helping others. Since Jesus is our savior, I can't understand why we don't know what **is necessary** for Him. That is so important God uses this amount of scripture to explain! It appears to have been hidden for the last two thousand years. What **is necessary** for him?

For more than thirty-five years, I have helped people with money through mortgage loans, life insurance, investments, estate planning, retirement-income planning, or wealth management. Over the years, I've been asked many theological questions about finance, such as "What about the mark of the beast [666]?" "Can a man be wealthy in the world's eyes and still be saved?" and "Isn't tithing just an Old Testament law that I don't need to practice?"

I've also read a number of books on Christian money management; some were good, and others were bad. I tore up the worst one before I threw it in the garbage. It tried to convince its readers that tithing is no longer scriptural. When I looked up the verses they quoted, I found that all of them were being used only partially or being given the author's own interpretations that did not match what the Word actually says.

Instead of reading other books, I felt that the only way I could honestly answer questions about money was to read *the* book—the Bible. I knew I could trust God's Word, so I didn't have to figure out who was right or wrong. If it can't be backed up by the Word, it's worthless.

In my early years, I never heard anyone argue about what is in the Old Testament. It was always "Tithing is not in the New Testament." We must remember that the Bible works as a whole and never contradicts itself. To refute that idea—that tithing is purely an Old Testament command—I decided that most of this book will cover the New Testament's truths about tithing.

What drew me to the idea of tithing was something that had me really puzzled: I couldn't understand why only a few people had peace even when they experienced trials. Some of these people were poor, and others were wealthy; to these few, how little or how much they had made no difference. There was a sense of peace that surrounded them. It was palpable. I knew that it was the kind of peace I wanted.

I developed such a thirst for the answers for these questions that I quit putting them off. I kept thinking, *What a task it would be to study that much! Who am I? Why would anyone read what I have to say?* Using the Scriptures, I came to realize I wasn't the one who was talking. I am merely presenting what God's Word has to say on the matter of money.

In my studies, I learned that if we're not giving Christ what is necessary, essential, or needful or—as the Complete Jewish Bible (CJB) puts it—what Jesus "has to have" (and those words are only used together once in the entire version), we may need to reevaluate our walk with the Lord. Tithing and other works do not earn our salvation (Christ has already paid that price for us), but they do serve as checkpoints where we can stop and ask ourselves, "Did I really accept Christ? If so, why am I not obeying His words?"

I hope that you do truly love Jesus and simply have not been told the whole truth—what I call the shocking truth. I say "shocking" because the truth has been in the New Testament for over two thousand years. And guess what? There are over seventy biblical rewards that can be bestowed upon us when we are obedient to the Word of God. As we get started in this discussion, take a look at these verses from His Word, which I'll expound in the coming chapters:

But, beloved, we are confident of better things concerning you, yes, things that accompany salvation, though we speak in this manner. For God is not unjust to forget your work and labor of love which you have shown toward His name, in that you have ministered to the saints, and do minister. And we desire that each one of you show the same diligence to the full assurance of hope until the end, **that you do not become sluggish**, but imitate those who through faith and patience inherit the promises. (Heb. 6:9–12)

All the nations will be gathered before Him, and He will separate them one from another, as a shepherd divides his sheep from the goats. And He will set the sheep on His right hand, but the goats on the left. Then the King will say to those on His right hand, "Come, you blessed of My Father, inherit the kingdom prepared for you from the foundation of the world: for I was hungry and you gave Me food; I was thirsty and you gave Me drink; I was a stranger and you took Me in; I was naked and you clothed Me; I was sick and you visited Me; I was in prison and you came to Me." Then the righteous will answer Him, saying, "Lord, when did we see You hungry and feed You, or thirsty and give You drink? When did we see You a stranger and take You in, or naked and clothe You? Or when did we see You sick, or in prison, and come to You?" And the King will answer and say to them, **"Assuredly, I say to you, in as much as you did it to one of the least of these My brethren, you did it to Me."** (Matt. 25:32–40)

Therefore, do not let your good be spoken of as evil; for the kingdom of God is not eating and drinking, but righteousness and peace and joy in the Holy Spirit. **For he who serves Christ in these things is acceptable to God** and approved by men. (Rom. 14:16–18)

Jesus answered and said to him, "If anyone loves Me, he will keep My word; and My Father will love him, and We will come to him and make Our home with him. He who does not love Me does not keep My words; and the word which you hear is not Mine but the Father's who sent Me." (John 14:23–24)

For whatever things were written before **were written for our learning**, that we through the patience **and comfort of the Scriptures might have hope.** (Rom. 15:4)

I pray that you will find this the most extensive and comprehensive book on the subject of money that you have ever read—except for the Word itself, of course. We must have a good foundation of who we are in Christ. We are all servants. *How many of you would continue to pay a servant who didn't do what you asked?* Let's all look to the future of how many more that may go home with us by supporting our Christian workers, as Jesus asked.

CHAPTER 1

First Things First: Tithing

According to *Webster's College Dictionary*, the *tithe* is "a tenth of goods or income paid as a tax for the support of the church." According to the Bible, the tithe is a tenth of *any* increase.

What about the Old Testament law? The trouble with the tithe is that it was first introduced in the Old Testament. In my years of working mostly with Christians regarding their investments, retirement-income planning, and estate planning, I have often heard that tithing was part of the Old Testament, which Jesus did away with. But consider this: "Then Melchizedek king of Salem brought out bread and wine; he was the priest of God Most High. And he blessed him and said: 'Blessed be Abram of God Most High, Possessor of heaven and earth; and blessed be God Most High, Who has delivered your enemies into your hand.' And he gave him a tithe of **all**" (Gen. 14:20). Thank God that we have tried to stop slavery as people were included in this example as part of the tithe! This story in Genesis occurred 430 years before the Old Testament law was even introduced. How can something that came 430 years before the law be done away with (because we are no longer "under the law") when it wasn't part of the law in the first place?

It's true that offerings are mentioned in the Old Testament, but does this mean that we aren't commanded to offer them anymore? We know that Christ Jesus took the place of the sin offerings—the blood sacrifice—but He did not do away with tithes, vow offerings, or freewill offerings. I don't know about you, but I would like to continue to **rejoice in all I put my hands to**. I also want my **household to rejoice**. Two of the seventy rewards for doing as Jesus asked!

I have also been told that tithing was a Jewish practice and not applicable to Christians today. Please consider this: God calls Jewish people His chosen people, and we are grafted into Christ when we accept Jesus as our Lord. If it was considered a godly practice for the Jews, and we are now grafted in with the Jews, why would it not be a godly practice for us today? Tithing is just as important today, especially when you consider *who* is being blessed now. Plus, according to the Bible, there are more than seventy spiritual rewards that can result from giving beyond the duty of the tithe. Why would anyone risk losing even one these spiritual rewards? Why would it no longer be necessary for the maintenance of God's workers when all that changed was there are no longer blood sacrifices, which was the only thing Jesus did away with by His blood.

The one in ten who tithe are doing it out of love for Jesus, and there can be no better reason. You are the ones Jesus needs to help teach those who are still on milk. They need the solid food of God's Word, which is the only way to stop the wolves from lying about tithing and calling good teachers, and pastor thieves! There is way more on the Internet and YouTube against tithing than for tithing. If we don't stand for all of God's Word, what chance do our children and grandchildren have when their leaders don't teach the full truth, which sets us free?

What if I can't afford to tithe?

Old Testament law or not, **money** is a major reason why Christians neglect tithing. **You may not have money, but you do have time; that could replace money**. Consider this: a godly evangelist once told me that parents today are advising their children not to go into ministry work because ministry work is not being supported financially. Many Christians neglect to tithe because they think they can't afford it and fear losing their financial security, but at what cost? <u>If we fail to support the work of the Lord and His</u>

ministers, *we are part of the reason that Christianity is declining in America.* Where is the evidence that accompanies salvation (Heb. 6:9)?

Christ Himself set an example for us by tithing! (Matt. 17:27) If you are merely using your mouth to proclaim that you're a Christian while not honoring Christ by doing what He did, I have to question your love for Christ. **The only way you can truly proclaim your love for Christ is by obeying and following Him.** Jesus said, "But why do you call Me 'Lord, Lord,' and not do the things which I say?" (Luke 6:46). In the verses at the end of this book's introduction, Jesus is referring to the people who thought they could pick and choose the parts of the Scriptures that they were willing to obey. These same people are the ones who believe the wolf in sheep's clothing. The wolf tells them that tithing is not necessary for Christians today instead of what God actually said.

> Beware of false prophets, who come to you in sheep's clothing, but inwardly they are ravenous wolves. You will know them by their fruits. (Matt. 7:15–16)

> Therefore, I testify to you this day that **I am innocent of the blood of all men**. **For** I have not shunned to declare to you the **whole** counsel of God. Therefore take heed to yourselves and to all the flock, among which the Holy Spirit has made you overseers, to shepherd the church of God which He purchased with His own blood. For I know this, that after my departure savage wolves will come in among you, not sparing the flock. Also from among yourselves men will rise up, **speaking perverse things, to draw away the disciples after themselves**. Therefore watch and remember that **for three years I did not cease to warn everyone night and day with tears.** (Acts 20:26–31)

For a good tree does not bear bad fruit, nor does a bad tree bear good fruit. For every tree is known by its own fruit. For men do not gather figs from thorns, nor do they gather grapes from a bramble bush. A good man out of the good treasure of his heart brings forth good; and an evil man out of the evil treasure of his heart brings forth evil. For out of the abundance of the heart his mouth speaks. (Luke 6:43–45)

Consider these verses from the Old Testament:

The burden of the word of the Lord **to Israel** by Malachi. (Mal 1:1)

You are cursed with a curse, for you have robbed Me, **Even this whole nation.** (Mal. 3:9)

The above two scriptures prove that Malachi was not written just for the priests, as the wolves lie about! Another way to spot a wolf is when they try to create uncertainty about Jacob's tithe in the following verses.

"Behold, I am with you and will keep you wherever you go, and will bring you back to this land; for I will not leave you until I have done what I have spoken to you." Then Jacob awoke from his sleep and said, "Surely the Lord is in this place, and I did not know it." And he was afraid and said, "How awesome is this place! This is none other than the house of God, and this is the gate of heaven!"

Then Jacob rose early in the morning and took the stone that he had put at his head, set it up as a pillar, and poured oil on top of it. And he called the name of that place Bethel; but the name of that city had been Luz previously. Then Jacob made a vow, saying, "If God will be with me, and keep me in this way that I am going, and give me bread to eat and clothing to put on, so that I come back to my father's house in peace, then the Lord shall be my God. And this stone which I have set as a pillar shall be God's house, **and of all** that You give me I will surely give a tenth to You." (Gen. 28:15–22)

They try to create doubt with "If God"—as if Jacob could ever have uncertainty or doubt in God. Since God said it, Jacob was sure about God's word; **he was already building God's house**. Of course, he didn't owe a tithe until he received an increase. This is the only thing that is conditional about the tithe—no increase, no tithe. God told him the increase was coming. By the way, I pray that God will give me an advance notice like that!

The third way the wolves try to create doubt is to say Abraham never tithed or never tithed from his personal belongings. They must have overlooked the following

Because Abraham obeyed My voice and kept My charge, My commandments, My statutes, and My laws. (Gen. 26:5)

You have just read three ways the wolves are trying to use to mislead unknowing Christians. The main way they lie is by rewording or using partial scriptures, like Satan tried to do with Jesus! Anyone trying to use even one of the above verses to say that tithing is not scriptural today should be shunned. **They are either wolves or have believed a wolf instead of God's Word.** If anyone disagrees, ask for copy-and-paste, not their opinion. You want what God says, not a man's opinion!

"A son honors his father, and a servant his master. **If then I am the Father**, **where is My honor**?

And **if I am a Master**, where is My reverence?" says the Lord of hosts to you priests who despise My name. "Yet you say, 'In what way have we despised Your name?' You offer defiled food on My altar. But say, 'In what way have we defiled You?' By saying, 'The table of the Lord is contemptible.' And when you offer the blind as a sacrifice, is it not evil? And when you offer the lame and sick, is it not evil? Offer it then to your governor! Would he be pleased with you? Would he accept you favorably?" says the Lord of hosts. **"But now entreat God's favor,** that He may be gracious to us. While this is being done by your hands, will He accept you favorably?" says the Lord of hosts. "Who is there even among you who would shut the doors, so that you would not kindle fire on My altar in vain? I have no pleasure in you," says the Lord of hosts, "nor will I accept an offering from your hands. For from the rising of the sun, even to its going down, My name shall be great among the Gentiles; in every place incense shall be offered to My name, **and a pure offering**; for My name shall be great among the nations," says the Lord of hosts. "But you profane it, in that you say, 'The table of the Lord is defiled; and its fruit, its food, is contemptible.' You also say, 'Oh, what a weariness!' and you sneer at it," says the Lord of hosts. "And you bring the stolen, the lame, and the sick; thus you bring an offering! Should I accept this from your hand?" says the Lord. "But cursed be the deceiver who has in his flock a male, and takes a vow, but sacrifices to the Lord what is blemished—for I am a great King," says the Lord of hosts, **"and My name is to be feared among the nations."** (Mal. 1:6–14)

"And now, O priests, this commandment is for you. If you will not hear, and if you will not take it to heart, to give glory to My name," says the Lord of hosts, "I will send a curse upon you, and I will curse your blessings. Yes, I have cursed them already, because you do not take it to heart. Behold, I will rebuke your descendants, and spread refuse on your faces, the refuse of your solemn feasts; and one will take you away with it. Then you shall know that I have sent this commandment to you, **that My covenant with Levi may continue**," says the Lord of hosts. "My covenant was with him, one of life and peace, and I gave them to him **that he might fear Me; so he feared Me and was reverent before My name**. The law of truth was in his mouth, and injustice was not found on his lips. He walked with Me in peace and equity, **and turned many away from iniquity**. For the lips of a priest should keep knowledge, and people should seek the law from his mouth; for he is the messenger of the Lord of hosts. But you have departed from the way; you have caused many to stumble at the law. You have corrupted the covenant of Levi," says the Lord of hosts. "Therefore, I also have made you contemptible and base before all the people, because you have not kept My ways but have shown partiality in the law." (Mal. 2:1–9)

"Behold, I send My messenger, and He will prepare the way before Me. And the Lord, whom you seek, will suddenly come to His temple, even the Messenger of the covenant, in whom you delight. Behold, He is coming," says the Lord of hosts. "But who can endure the day of His coming? And who can stand when He appears? For

He is like a refiner's fire and like launderers' soap. He will sit as a refiner and a purifier of silver; He will purify the sons of Levi, and purge them as gold and silver, that they may offer to the Lord an offering in righteousness." (Mal. 3:1–3)

These passages discuss what Jesus will do, and there's no way that He will come back only for the sons of Levi.

"Then [after Jesus] the offering of Judah and Jerusalem will be pleasant to the Lord, as in the days of old, as in former years. And I will come near you for judgment; I will be a swift witness against sorcerers, against adulterers, against perjurers, against those who exploit wage earners and widows and orphans, and against those who turn away an alien—**because they do not fear Me**," says the Lord of hosts. "For I am the Lord, I do not change; therefore, you are not consumed, O sons of Jacob. Yet from [since or after] the days of your fathers you have gone away from My ordinances and have not kept them. **Return to Me, and I will return to you**," says the Lord of hosts. "But you said, 'In what way shall we return?'" (Mal. 3:4–7)

Will a man rob God? Yet you have robbed Me! But you say, "In what way have we robbed You?" **In tithes and offerings**. You are cursed with a curse, for you have robbed Me, **even this whole nation.** (Mal. 3:8–9)

I've heard some say that God was only speaking to the Jewish nation of that time—That means the rest of the world doesn't have to pay attention to His Word, and we don't have to either. Again, the word *even* in the above context means "including this nation."

Was God only speaking to the Jews of that time? If that's so, then Malachi's third chapter has been worthless for approximately 2,400 years. Malachi was written approximately 400 years before Christ. Christ died and rose approximately 2,000 years ago. Since many Jews do not believe that Christ is the Messiah, Malachi's third chapter would be worthless to them. So was it only written for the Jews of that time and not for the Jews of today or for those of us who are grafted in?

In verses six and eight, God says we've robbed Him of His tithes and offerings. Tithing is a wage owed to the church—a duty. Romans 4:4 says that for him who works, wages are not counted as grace but as a debt. Why would anyone expect to be rewarded for paying a debt? Remember, the definition of *tithe* is "a tax for the support of the church." Why would God be speaking *only* to the people of that time, as I've heard some say? If that were the case, why not throw out the entire Old Testament? Why did the Holy Spirit make sure it was written down for us today?

> Then those **who feared** the Lord spoke to one another, and the Lord listened and heard them; so a book of remembrance was written before Him **for those who fear the Lord** and who meditate on His name. "They shall be Mine," says the Lord of hosts, "on the day that I make them My jewels. And I will spare them, as a man **spares his own son who serves him**." Then you shall again discern, between the righteous and the wicked, **between one who serves God and one who does not serve Him**." (Mal. 3:16–18)

If the wolves are right, if Malachi really was only for the priests, it would appear the book of remembrance was only for the priests!

What better way to wrap up the Old Testament's last book than with a reference to the New Testament that is about to come?

We, as believers, are in debt to those who do ministry work, and far too many of us are looking for ways to get out of paying our debt.

Every time I turn around, I hear someone say, "I don't have enough. I have trouble with paying my bills." With only one in ten tithing, it's no wonder we hear that all the time! Perhaps you don't have enough because you're using it all for your own benefit. You are missing the rewards, which are at least seventy, and I will soon discuss them. There are many, many rewards that start after you give the tithe!

Most Christians assume that a tithe is purely money, but did you know that Christ desires our time too? **Using your time and/or money to help others gets you included in the rewards!** Jesus said, "Woe to you, scribes and Pharisees, hypocrites! For you pay tithe of mint and anise and cumin, and have neglected the weightier matters of the law: justice and mercy and faith. These you ought to have done, **without leaving the others undone**" (Matt. 23:23). Some say that Jesus here was talking only to the scribes and the Pharisees who were under the Mosaic Law and that He used this reasoning so as not to offend them. I believe that being called a hypocrite would offend most people. I cannot believe that there were no Christians in the audience. Why would Jesus's words be included here when He was crucified a short time after He spoke these words? Do His words here not count anymore after His death and resurrection? Jesus spoke about **taking time** to show justice, mercy, and faith as being part of the law. Should we also ignore this part today? We don't get to take out the parts of the Scriptures that we don't like and only obey what we do like. You could *try* to take something out, but that doesn't nullify its truth. You're only hurting yourself when you disobey the Lord.

Please be careful that you're not teaching others not to tithe. I know that what I'm going to say next will offend people who believe that the tithe is enough, but you will be shocked to know how many blessings begin after the giving of the tithes. To be sure, it is a great blessing here on earth for those who receive the tithe in return for their ministry work. It's a payment—a debt owed for their labor. There are only a few of us who can afford to work without pay. Jesus also said, "But woe to you Pharisees! For you tithe mint and rue and all manner of herbs, and pass by justice and the love of God. These you ought, to have done, **without leaving the others undone**" (Luke 11:42).

The way we show God our love is by doing what He asks us to do—be obedient. Jesus also spoke this parable (a short allegorical story designed to illustrate or teach religious principle) to those who were trusting in themselves, thinking they were righteous in tithes while withholding mercy to others:

> Two men went up to the temple to pray, one a Pharisee and the other a tax collector. The Pharisee stood and prayed thus with himself, "God, I thank You that I am not like other men—extortioners, unjust, adulterers, or even as this tax collector. I fast twice a week; I give tithes of all that I possess." And the tax collector, standing afar off, would not so much as raise his eyes to heaven, but beat his breast, saying, "God, be merciful to me, a sinner!" I tell you, this man went down to his house justified rather than the other; for everyone who exalts himself will be humbled, and he who humbles himself will be exalted. (Luke 18:10–14)

The Pharisee in the above parable tried to use tithes to prove that he was righteous. But this does not justify anyone, especially when it is done for attention or for the approval of other men. What God wanted from this Pharisee was his time—time to be merciful and enact godly character in his life.

Think about the previous passage in light of the old argument: "But tithing is just for Old Testament Jews." If we use this excuse and think that it no longer counts, then we would have to say we can also bypass justice and the love of God. But why would Jesus say something today that would not mean anything tomorrow? Jesus said that whoever takes time to humble himself will be exalted. What a blessing!

Also consider this verse: "You who say not to commit adultery, do you commit adultery [are you unchaste in action or in thought]? You who abhor and loathe idols, do you rob temples [do you appropriate to your own use what is consecrated to God, thus robbing the sanctuary and doing sacrilege]?" (Rom. 2:22, AMP).

The tithe is consecrated to God. I've heard some say that this verse doesn't use the word *tithe*, but what else is there in the sanctuary that is consecrated to God that we could rob him of—thereby doing sacrilege?

> Now concerning the collection for the saints, as I have given orders to the churches of Galatia, so you must do also: on the first day of the week let each one of you lay something aside, storing up as he may prosper, that there be no collections when I come. And when I come, whomever you approve by your letters I will send to bear your gift to Jerusalem. (1 Cor. 16:1–3)

Is not the definition of *tithe* "a tenth part of goods or income paid as a tax for the support of the church"? I thought support was what the tithe was for! If the collection was not the tithe, I guess we now know that there were two collections—one for support and another one for support! Well, okay! It's all His anyway! Are the saints not the leaders and workers in the church? The above verses say that "**you must do also**," but please notice that it also says "as [you] may prosper." How can you prosper if you don't have an increase from work or money of some kind? Paul was talking to the church in Corinth and said that he gave the same order to the churches in Galatia. These were all Christian churches.

If you still choose to believe that Paul was not referring to the tithe, you in any case have to acknowledge that he did say "a collection for saints on the first day of the week." Why would the inspired Word of God only be talking to the Christian churches of the past? "For the love of Christ compels us, because we judge thus: that if One died for all, then all died; and He died for all, **that those who live should live no longer for themselves**, but for Him who died for them and rose again" (2 Cor. 5:14–15).

I believe that the book of Hebrews could be retitled *The Tithe Book*. I am so bold as to say that anyone who is reading this will agree with God's Word by the end of this chapter, while remembering the scripture is copy and paste, not my opinion; It's God's word—even if you have been struggling with it up to this point. (Please remember, Hebrews was written approximately sixty-five years after Christ died and rose.)

Hebrews 1:1–4: "God, who at various times and in various ways spoke in time past to the fathers by the prophets, **has** in these last days spoken to us by His Son, whom He has appointed heir of all things, through whom also He made the worlds; who being the brightness of His glory and the express image of His person, and upholding all things by the word of His power, when He **had** by Himself purged our sins, sat down at the right hand of the Majesty on high, **having become** so much better than the angels, as **He has by inheritance obtained a more excellent name than they.**

We know that Jesus *permanently*, once and for all, took care of the sacrifices for our sins (i.e., He purged them). When we ask for forgiveness in His name **and** make Him Lord in our lives, we get to spend eternity with Him. But He is not your Lord if you are not doing what He has asked you to do.

Consider also the following verses from Hebrews **(they are all building up to the very important truth of Hebrews 8:3):**

Hebrews 2:1–2: "**Therefore** we must give the more earnest heed to the things we have heard, lest we drift away. For if the word spoken through angels proved steadfast, and every transgression and disobedience received a just reward."

Hebrews 2:17–18: "**Therefore**, in all things He had to be made like His brethren, that He might be a merciful and faithful High Priest in things pertaining to God, to make propitiation for the sins of the people."

Hebrews 3:1–6: "**Therefore**, holy brethren, partakers of the heavenly calling, consider the Apostle and High Priest of our confession, Christ Jesus, **who was faithful** to Him who appointed Him, as Moses also was faithful in all His house. **For this One has been counted worthy of more glory than Moses**, in as much as He who built the house has more honor than the house. For every house is built by someone, but He who built all things is God. And Moses indeed was faithful in all His house as a servant, for a testimony of those things which would be spoken afterward, but Christ as a Son over His own house, whose house we are **if we hold fast the confidence and the rejoicing of the hope firm to the end.**"

Hebrews 3:9–10: "And saw My works forty years. Therefore I was angry with that generation, and said, 'They always go astray in their heart, **and they have not known My ways.**'"

Hebrews 3:18–19: "And to whom did He swear that they would not enter His rest, but **to those who did not obey**? So we see that they could not enter in because of unbelief."

Seventy different biblical blessings starting with Matthew through Revelation for knowing and obeying His ways! Please see chapter five.

Hebrews 4:1–2: "**Therefore**, since a promise remains of entering His rest, let us fear lest any of you seem to have come short of it. For indeed the gospel was **preached to us as well as to them**; but the word which they heard did not profit them, **not being mixed** with faith in those who heard it."

Hebrews 4:14–16: "Seeing then that **we have a great high priest**, **that is passed into the heavens**, Jesus the Son of God, let us hold fast our profession. For **we have** not a High Priest which cannot be touched with the feeling of our infirmities; but was in all points tempted like as we are, yet without sin. Let us therefore come boldly unto the throne of grace, that we may obtain mercy, and find grace to help in time of need."

Hebrews 5:1: "For every high priest taken from among men is appointed for men in things pertaining to God, that he may offer **both** gifts and sacrifices for sins."

Hebrews 5:5–6: "So also Christ glorified not himself **to be made a High Priest**; but he that said unto him, Thou art my Son, today have I begotten thee. As he saith also in another place, Thou art a priest for ever after the order of Melchisedec."

Hebrews 5:9–14: "**And having been perfected**, **He became** the author of eternal salvation **to all who obey Him**, called by God as High Priest 'according to the order of Melchizedek,' **of whom we have much to say**, and hard to explain, <u>since you have become dull of hearing</u>. For though <u>by this time you ought to be teachers</u>, you need someone to teach you again the first principles of the oracles of God; and **you have come to need milk and not solid food**. For everyone who partakes only of milk is unskilled in the word of righteousness, for he is a babe. But solid food belongs to those who are of full age, that is, those **who by reason of use** have their senses exercised to discern both good and evil.

We're reminded to obey Him by following His Word. I don't know if you're like me, but before I truly knew the Word, there were many times my discernment was not good enough to protect me from evils—such as people who lied to me and misled me by the use of partial scriptures. We must feast on God's Word so that we can grow and understand the rich fullness of all He desires from us—**not be babies who only take the milk** and not the meat!

Hebrews 6:1–3: "**Therefore, leaving the discussion of the elementary principles of Christ**, let us go on to perfection, not laying again the foundation of repentance from dead works and of faith toward God, of the doctrine of baptisms, of laying on of hands, of resurrection of the dead, and of eternal judgment. And this we will do if God permits."

If we quit school after elementary, we will miss a lot. What good is the foundation without the building? We have just been told by God that there is something so important that He refers to "faith toward God, of the doctrine of baptisms, of laying on of hands, of resurrection of the dead, and of eternal judgment" **as elementary**.

Hebrews 6:9–12: "But, beloved, we are confident of **better things** concerning you, yes, **things that accompany salvation**, though we speak in this manner. For God is not unjust to forget your work and labor of love which you have shown toward His name, in that you **have ministered to the saints, and do minister**. And we desire that each one of you show the same diligence to the full assurance of hope until the end, that you do **not become slug-gish**, but imitate those who through faith and patience inherit the promises."

Hebrews 6:18–20: "That by two immutable things, in which it was impossible for God to lie, we might have a strong consolation, who have fled for refuge to lay hold upon the hope set before us: Which hope we have as an anchor of the soul, both sure and stead-fast, and which entereth into that within the veil; Whither the **fore-runner is for us entered, even Jesus, made a High Priest for ever after the order of Melchisedec.**"

The number-one way we minister to the saints, of course, is to provide for their needs. This can come from time and money spent serving Jesus. There are at least seventy spiritual rewards that follow our giving time and money in service to others, especially in the ser-vice of the saints.

Hebrews 7:1–2: "For this Melchizedek, king of Salem, priest of the Most High God, who met Abraham returning from the slaughter of the kings and blessed him, to whom also Abraham **gave a tenth part of all**, first being translated 'king of righteousness,' and then also king of Salem, meaning 'king of peace.'"

Hebrews 7:4: "Now consider how great this man was, to whom even the patriarch Abraham gave a **tenth of the spoils.**"

Hebrews 7:8: "Here mortal men receive tithes, but there He receives them, of whom it is witnessed that He lives."
(ONLY JESUS HAS BEEN WITNESSED TO LIVE, SO THIS HAS TO BE REFERRING TO JESUS IN HEAVEN.)

The unsaved are giving tithes to priests who die, and the saved are giving tithes to Jesus through His workers.

Hebrews 7:15–17: "And it is yet far more evident if, in the likeness of Melchizedek, there arises another priest **who has come**, not according to the law of a fleshly commandment, **but according to the power of an endless life**. For He testifies: 'You are a priest forever According to the order of Melchizedek.'"

Hebrews 7:23–28: "Also there were many priests, because they were prevented by death from continuing. But He, because He continues forever, has an unchangeable priesthood. Therefore He is also able to save to the uttermost those who come to God through Him, since He always lives to make intercession for them. For such a High Priest was fitting for us, who is holy, harmless, undefiled, separate from sinners, and **has** become higher than the heavens; **who does not need daily**, as those high priests, to offer up sacrifices, first for His own sins and then for the people's, for this He **did once for all when He offered up Himself**. For the law appoints as high priests men who have weakness, **but the word of the oath**, **which came after the law**, appoints the Son who has been perfected forever."

To this day, I continue to thank God for bringing to my remembrance verse 25 when I needed it for my grandmother. Being of American Indian descent (of which I am very proud), she was raised for the first eight years of her life on the Nez Perce reservation in Idaho. One Friday night, I called my grandmother and asked her if there was anything that she would like me to pick up for her because if she had time, I would like to talk with her in the morning. Of course, she said yes. That night, it seemed like I kept getting busier and busier and almost called my grandmother to delay my visit. When I arrived that Saturday morning (I can still see my grandmother sitting across the living room), she asked me what I wanted to talk about.

I asked my grandmother if she had ever received Jesus. She replied, "Do you mean the white man's God?"

"Grandma, you know better than that!" I said.

Then she asked me if I was perfect.

"Grandma, you know I'm not."

The Holy Spirit prompted me to ask her if she had ever heard that Jesus lives to intercede for those who come to him. She answered yes.

"If we were perfect," I told her, "He would not need to intercede for us."

She accepted Jesus that Saturday morning. When she died on Monday morning, before I could make it to the hospital, she entered our eternal home in heaven because Jesus interceded for her.

> For such a High Priest was fitting for us, who is holy, harmless, undefiled, separate from sinners, and has become higher than the heavens; who does not need daily, as those high priests, to offer up sacrifices, first for His own sins and then for the people's, for this He did once for all when He offered up Himself. For the law appoints as high priests men who have weakness, but the word of the oath, <u>which came after the law</u>, appoints the Son who has been perfected forever. (Heb. 7:26–28)

Please notice that this says "after the law." So even if you thought that tithing was in the law and doesn't apply anymore, you must now admit that tithing *was pre-law* and *post-law*. Again, Hebrews was written approximately sixty-five years after Christ died. It spoke to Christians of that time, and it speaks to us today.

And here's the point:

Hebrews 8:1–3: "**Now this is the main point of the things we are saying**: We **have** such a High Priest, **who is seated** at the right hand of the throne of the Majesty in the heavens, a Minister of the sanctuary and of the true tabernacle which the Lord erected, and not man. For every high priest is appointed to offer **both** gifts and sacrifices [Jesus was the last blood sacrifice]. **Therefore, it is necessary that this One also have something to offer.**"

Yes, folks, it says *necessary*. At this point, some might still say that "something to offer" doesn't talk about the tithe. But remember that in Hebrews 7:8, the word *them* was used instead of *tithes*. Here it says that Christ must also "have something to offer."

In twenty-seven of thirty different Bible versions, I checked the use of the word *is* in Hebrews 8:3. Leading up to the verse, some of the comments were "We have much to say!" "Hard to understand!" "Become dull of hearing!" "Should have understood by now!" "Don't stay on milk!" and "By reason of use!"

Three versions decided to use the past-tense *was*—what *was* necessary for Jesus. How could you have accepted Christ without already knowing this? Milk of the word! He is the Son of God! He "was" the last, perfect blood sacrifice.

I prefer to believe the other twenty-seven versions that ask what *is* necessary since we have been using the present tense in the seven chapters that lead up to this point. Yes, examples of the past are used to show that if it's needed then, it's needed now. What is necessary for my Creator? He doesn't need my money, which is technically already His! How could He need anything? Things that accompany salvation! (Heb. 6:9). Our obedience produces the fruit that accompanies!

The word of God just took seven chapters to tell us how important Melchizedek **was** while reminding us how much more important our Lord Jesus **is**. The only reason to talk about Melchizedek was the tithe—the 10 percent. We are stealing from God if we do not tithe (Mal. 3:8). The tithe can be the only answer! The money in the hands of the workers is the only thing that could be necessary!

This is why it's so important to consider the verses that precede and follow a verse in the Scriptures. As for the scripture following Hebrews 8:3, it can only be used to confirm what was summarized, as the answers were already given. It is also important to read the other scriptures pertaining to the same subject. In the verses leading up to this point, it clearly talks about the tithe because that's what is meant by a tenth. The only reason Melchizedek was brought into this conversation was because of the tithe and to remind us that even though he was a great man, Jesus is even more so. If you are not convinced that this is proof that tithing is very important today, I don't know what else to say! I do not know how God's Word could be read any differently, especially when you consider who it's for in Hebrews 8:3 and while remembering Hebrews 7:8. It said the tithe is for Jesus.

Furthermore, I choose to believe that it should make you want to give more than the tithe. If it's "necessary" that Jesus "has to have," how can we consider giving him less than old Melchizedek? Will you continue to shortchange the Lord? Before you answer that question, consider this: What will your rewards be in heaven? As far as I'm concerned, anyone who says tithing is not for today is a wolf in sheep's clothing that will lead you astray willfully **or because he also has been led astray**. It's bad enough for a person to lose his own rewards in heaven, but to cause others to lose theirs is even worse. What God says to do, we *must* do. We must support the ministry before it's too late.

When I checked the Old and New Testaments of other Bible versions, the words *necessary, essential,* and *needful* were used very few times. Hebrews 8:3 in the New King James Version uses the word *necessary*. A few others use the words *essential* or *needful*. I found it very interesting that in the Complete Jewish Bible, the words *"has to have"* are used, and that phrase is only used once in the whole Complete Jewish Bible. He gave His life for us. How can we even think of giving Him less than what would've been given to Melchizedek?

Therefore, since we are receiving a kingdom which cannot be shaken, let us have grace, by which **we may serve God acceptably with reverence and godly fear**. For our God is a consuming fire. (Heb. 12:28–29)

These are grumblers, complainers, walking according to their own lusts; and they mouth great swelling words, flattering people to gain advantage. But you, beloved, remember the words which were spoken before by the apostles of our Lord Jesus Christ: <u>how they told you that there would be mockers in the last time who would walk according to their own ungodly lusts</u>. These are sensual persons, who cause divisions, not having the Spirit. (Jude 16–19)

But you, beloved, building yourselves up on your most holy faith, praying in the Holy Spirit, keep yourselves in the love of God, looking for the mercy of our Lord Jesus Christ unto eternal life. And on some have compassion, making a distinction; **but others save with fear, pulling them out of the fire**, hating even the garment defiled by the flesh. (Jude 20–23)

Now to Him who is able to keep you from stumbling, and to present you faultless before the presence of His glory with exceeding joy, to God our Savior, Who alone is wise, be glory and majesty, dominion and power, both now and forever. Amen. (Jude 24–25)

Kingdom benefits for teaching the tithe is necessary for Jesus, and necessary ***does not*** mean "under law"!

1. God receives the honor due to Him.
2. There are way too many people who feel Christian leaders beg for money. People even leave churches that talk too much about money. There are divorces over tithing, including myself, having gone through one over the tithe that her priest said I'm crazy if I believe necessary. Just teach full truth about the tithe from Gods words and we learn "necessary" for our Savior, we will want to give more time and/or money.
3. Stop the savage wolves from devouring the sheep like they are doing on the Internet when they say tithing is not scriptural. Not speaking the full truth is helping the wolves in their slaughter!
4. God's workers get paid so they can afford to work.
5. Jesus "was" the perfect blood sacrifice for sin? It's okay to say he still "is" since He can't be replaced!
6. Everyone needs and wants to belong to a group.
7. What God wants is our time; he wants it to produce fruit—the evidence that goes with us. Since **time is money, everyone** who wants to serve Jesus can do so without going into debt!
8. Don't go into debt to start tithing. Use your time to replace it.
9. **Using time, we can have many more workers help to expand the Kingdom at no out-of-pocket cost. How many more souls might be saved!**
10. It only takes forty-eight minutes over six days (4.8 hours a week). Your church knows who needs help.
11. Can you imagine how many more people would be helped if two out of ten tithed instead of only one. That's a 100% increase. So far I have not heard of any church who requires the tithe having financial problems, even though it should not be required. That would put tithe under a law.
12. **Really think about this! If no time/money is invested, it probably means very little to you.** We all pay more attention to something that we put time and/or money into.

13. We are reminded that everything is His in the first place.
14. We will not deny the good workers for fear the wolves will use it. It doesn't make sense to punish all the good workers for fear that a bad one might use it.
15. God's honor is necessary! **His honor should be the bottom line of your time**!
16. Those who don't have an increase for one reason or another can still count on receiving blessings as there are at least seventy different New Testament rewards for the use of time!
17. James 2:8: "If you really fulfill the **royal law** according to the Scripture, 'You shall love your neighbor as yourself,' you do well."
18. To anyone who disagrees, please only reply by using this scripture (copy and paste, NKJV):

CHAPTER 2

The Issue with Debt

You're probably thinking, "What if I don't have enough to give my tithe, let alone any offering above? Should I borrow to give to the Lord?"

Before I answer that, let's clear up a few things about debt. There's really nothing wrong with rightly using a credit card. Right before I accepted the Lord, I worked as a loan officer; I approved and collected loans. The man who trained me told me to never approve a loan for someone who says they are not worried about how they will pay their loan because the Lord will help them. My worldly trainer thought such a person could become a collection problem or might not even pay.

Since coming to know the Lord, I have heard people say that you should never borrow. If you use one or two scripture verses, you could possibly make that case, but if you read all the scriptures about borrowing, you will find that they don't say "Don't borrow." They *do* say that *if* you borrow, you need to be prepared to pay, even as a cosigner, and that it is best not to borrow at all. Using just a part of the Scriptures is like having all the ingredients for a great soup but leaving out one of the main ingredients. It just doesn't taste the same.

The conclusion I have come to as a money manager is that if it's done wisely, it's okay. Please be very careful because when you use money that the Lord has not yet given to you, **He is not obligated to pay**. If your car is working fine, why would you want to get into debt in order to buy a new car? If your television is working, why would you want to borrow money for a new TV? The savings in interest charges that you can get by paying cash can make a huge difference in your cash flow! Often you get a discount if you pay in cash.

I believe that a lot of advertising is from Satan. It's all about "You deserve this…," "You need this…," or "You must have it, or you won't be happy!" It's all about the *self*, and the *self* is the number-one tool that Satan uses to defeat us; he's been using it since the garden of Eden! Money used for material goods will never buy true, lasting happiness. **However, money and time that are used biblically can "buy" happiness that is eternal and lasting** and can provide many blessings while we're here on Earth.

I have also heard some people say that if we don't give, we will not receive. While this statement, in itself, is true, **please don't get caught up in the "give to get" mentality**, which is another one of Satan's tools. There are people who are so far in debt that they can't think straight, and you wouldn't want to end up like one of them.

This brings us back to our original question: "Should I go into debt to give offerings to the Lord?" I know some will argue this point, but I cannot believe **that God would want us to rob those whom we owe here on earth in order to give to Him**.

> Owe no one anything except to love one another, for he who loves another **has fulfilled the law**. For the commandments, "You shall not commit adultery," "You shall not murder," "You shall not steal," "You shall not bear false witness," "You shall not covet," and if there is any other commandment, are all summed up in this saying, namely, "You shall love your neighbor as yourself." Love does no harm to a neighbor; therefore love is the fulfillment of the law. (Rom. 13:8–10)

In my experience as a loan officer, the man who trained me had a negative opinion about Christians because they often didn't pay their debts. I can only imagine that in his mind, he thought, "If

Christians are so flaky, why would I want to become one?" If you are so far in debt that you feel you can't give money to the Lord's work, do not forget this: "Or do you despise the riches of His goodness, forbearance, and long-suffering, not knowing that the goodness of God leads you to repentance?" (Rom. 2:4).

Ask the Lord to forgive you and to help you develop a plan—in writing and preferably signed and dated (if you put it in writing, you will not forget that you have made a commitment to the Lord). As He helps you get rid of your debt, plan the amount you will start giving to Him. Then as you get rid of the debt, you can increase your giving. Notice that I said "as He helps you"; this means there has to be effort on your part. I believe that if you put it in writing, you will not forget that you have made a commitment to the Lord. I am certain that you'll be surprised by how fast He will help you get out of debt **if your real reason is to help Jesus** and not merely get out of debt. If you honor your commitment, you will not be using all your finances for the *self*, as you have in the past. Of course, in the meantime, work to replace the shortage.

Who knows? Paying your earthly debt may help bring salvation to that debt collector hounding you. You will also be ministering to the saints—even if it's not the full 10 percent that you owe (we serve a very loving and forgiving God, and He thankfully judges the intents of our hearts). **Giving to help bring others to the Lord so that you can receive more to give is the only "giving to get" that works**. If you truly want to be blessed, you must quit using it all for yourself. Remember that you can choose to be a slave to money or be a servant to God. "No servant can serve two **masters; for either he will hate the one and love the other, or else he will be loyal to the one and despise** the other. You cannot serve God and mammon" (Luke 16:13).

How we spend our time determines our reward. Most of us are given money in exchange for our work (of course, some are paid more than others). Money came into existence as a means of barter or exchange. It was easy to trade or barter with one's neighbor, but what if one needed perishable items like food or large items that were impractical to take on a long trip? It was easier to exchange one's work (one's time) or one's goods for money, which could then be used to buy needed goods elsewhere.

There have always been different forms of money because anything of value can be used as currency. Salt, gold, silver, precious gemstones, chickens, cows, horses, blankets, clothing, and food are some of the things that are used as money. All of these are being used as a form of money somewhere in the world today. I'm sure you can think of many other items that are used as a means of barter or exchange. And, again, your time has value. You may have heard this saying: "Time is money." Now you know that it is a valid statement. **The more wisdom and knowledge you have, the more valuable your time is.** The more valuable your time is, the more money, or the replacement of it, you can earn.

If I were a betting man (I believe it would be impossible to lose this bet), I would bet there is not one day that goes by in which you don't think about money in one way or another. I would even go so far as to say that some of us think more about money during the day than we do about the Lord. Guess what? You will receive the blessings or curses that have been earned by your use of the time and money that have been entrusted to your stewardship. It's your choice. But I'm sure you want the blessings. (I hope you can't wait to get to the section that discusses the seventy biblical rewards of time and money.) This must be why so much of the Scriptures talks about money and time and the use of them. In fact, it is the second-most talked-about subject in the New Testament—especially when you consider time and talent to be equal to money or a replacement for it. For those of you who have fallen on hard times, are out of work, or have fallen so far into debt that your creditors are bugging you, don't forget what Romans 2:4 says: "Or do you despise the riches of His goodness, forbearance, and long-suffering, not knowing that the goodness of God leads you to repentance?" This means that you can forget the past and look toward the future. The use of your time and talent is the only way to help the Lord bring more souls into His kingdom.

Some use their time and talent as a substitute for giving while earning money. As I discussed earlier, for those of you who have so much debt that you can't honor your earthly obligations and have made an agreement with the Lord for how you're going to increase your giving (knowing that money is just a replacement of your time), this can be good. You may really want to pray about this because the Word says we are to give the first fruits of all that we receive. Did you really give enough of your time to replace those first fruits? Leviticus 27:31 says, "If a man wants at all to redeem any of his tithes, he shall add one-fifth to it." This tells us that you have to add 20 percent to redeem the tithe.

For example, let's say that you're blessed with a forty-hour work-week. One-tenth of that, of course, is four hours. Four hours multiplied by sixty minutes equals 240 minutes. Twenty percent of 240 minutes is forty-eight minutes. So instead of just owing four hours, you need to spend four hours and forty-eight minutes to redeem your tithe.

I hope that this helps those who are deeply in debt to realize that there is hope. And don't forget whom the tithe blesses—your Lord and Savior, Jesus. Of course, if you have no increase, you have nothing to tithe. Let's say that at this point in time, you're only able to give 5 percent of your increase; then you would only owe 144 minutes to make up for the other 5 percent with your time. By the way, breaking 144 minutes down to a manageable time equals twenty-four minutes a day for six days. Less than half an hour a day!

If you are not helping others in some way, you could bring a curse upon yourself because you're not using your time as a proper steward of God. If you use it for yourself, how can you look forward to receiving a blessing? Of course, as I said before, don't forget what a loving, **forgiving** God we serve, and never give up on trying to bless Jesus.

Your tithe is part of your total giving. It's a starting point, the cornerstone—**<u>a debt you owe</u>**. It is like a membership fee to a club that you must pay in order to belong to it. Failing to tithe is like running red lights. You may be okay for a while, but sooner or later, you will pay for running those red lights! The more you rob God in your tithes and offerings, the greater the chance you have of bringing a curse upon yourself. Not receiving a blessing, in itself, is a curse.

Think about it. I'll say it again: Would it not be a curse *not* to receive a blessing promised by God as a reward for doing something He has asked you to do? And if you don't do what He has asked you to do, why should He reward you? Please give some thought to this. If the Lord has your money, though, He probably has the rest of you as well, and that can only bring a blessing.

Please remember that we are talking about eternal blessings here—not eternal life. Let this be clear: You cannot buy or work your way into heaven! The **full price for our sin debt has already been paid by Christ Jesus.**

Before I conclude this chapter, here is a quick note about gifts and inheritances. When you receive one or the other, remember that this is also considered an increase. Because my work involves helping people with their investments, retirement-income planning, insurance, and estate planning, I have talked with many attorneys who have told me that even though parents assumed their children would tithe out of their inheritances, they had yet to see one child do so. So the best example we can show our children, when we list them as beneficiaries, is to state that at least 10 percent should go to charity, thereby showing how important we feel the tithe is. (By the way, the vast majority of inheritances are gone in less than five years.)

Putting the tithe first helps remind us who we are living for. Those who are blessed with work look forward to being paid. Work usually takes up most of our day, but if we keep thinking about who we are working for, it keeps us more focused on the Lord throughout that time.

Never give up—no matter how many times you fail. If you give up, you're showing that you don't have faith in Jesus. The harder you have to work for something, the more you will appreciate it. It's time to get real. If you're not at least trying to tithe or do extra work with the 20 percent added, you don't believe what the Word of God says and may not really love Jesus.

Set a good, strong foundation for the use of money. You will surely be blessed, as the Word says. Let's all be good stewards so that more money can go into the Lord's work of helping others. Our first priority (which is also the best way to help others) is to bring the message of salvation through Christ Jesus to the lost. Yes, you need to feed and clothe them so that they feel your unconditional love, which will become a reflection of Jesus. That way, they will be more open to your reason for helping them. This is an excellent way to use our time and money to serve the Lord.

> Now may the God of peace who brought up our Lord Jesus from the dead, that great Shepherd of the sheep, through the blood of the everlasting covenant, make you complete in every good work **to do His will**, working in you what is well pleasing in His sight, through Jesus Christ, to whom be glory forever and ever. Amen. (Heb. 13:20–21)

> And let us not grow weary while doing good, for in due season we shall reap **if** we do not lose heart. Therefore, as we have opportunity, let us do good to all, especially to those who are of the household of faith. (Gal. 6:9–10)

CHAPTER 3

What about 666?

In this modern age of technology, there's a lot of talk about chip readers for credit cards and the possibility of getting chips implanted in our hands or someplace else. Christians who've read the book of Revelation tend to get uncomfortable with this because it sounds so much like the mark of the beast (666)! I have been asked about the mark of the beast more than most—probably because of my work with money. The book of Revelation tells us the following:

> He was granted power to give breath to the image of the beast, that the image of the beast should both speak and cause as many as would not worship the image of the beast to be killed. He causes all, both small and great, rich and poor, free and slave, to receive a mark on their right hand or on their foreheads, and that no one may buy or sell except one who has the mark or the name of the beast, or the number of his name. Here is wisdom. Let him who has understanding calculate the number of the beast, for it is the number of a man: his number is 666. (Rev. 13:15–18)

Let's zero in on the fact that the Word says that if you *don't* worship the beast, you will be killed. Why would the Word say this unless there are some people who will be killed? The only one who will have the courage to stand up to the beast will be a true Christian. A true Christian should *always* be willing to die for Christ at any time.

Many Christians are concerned that they may have unknowingly taken the mark of the beast. We serve a loving God. If you're truly worshipping Him, how could you be tricked into worshipping the beast? And what if you did somehow *accidentally* receive the mark of the beast (something that I still believe should not be possible)? That would be great! Now you'd be able to buy and sell, and you'd be in a position to help others who refused to worship the beast.

We must remember that it's not the mark that condemns you; it's the worship of the beast. There is no way you could get the mark without first worshipping the beast, and you cannot worship the beast unknowingly. Just like the conscious decision you made to accept Christ, you would have to consciously decide to worship the beast and receive the mark.

CHAPTER 4

Can a Christian Be Wealthy?

Over the years, I've had many people ask me if it's possible to be a wealthy Christian. Their questions aren't unfounded, especially when you consider verses like these: "Then Jesus said to his disciples, 'Assuredly, I say to you that it is hard for a rich man to enter the kingdom of heaven. And again I say to you, it is easier for a camel to go through the eye of a needle than for a rich man to enter the kingdom of God'" (Matt. 19:23–24).

But wait! If you stop there, you'll surely think that a wealthy person can't possibly be a Christian! That's why we have to keep the scripture in context. Look at the rest of the passage: "When His disciples heard it, they were greatly astonished, saying, 'Who then can be saved?' But Jesus looked at them and said to them, 'With men this is impossible, but **with God all things are possible**'" (Matt. 19:25–26).

Of course a person can be wealthy and a Christian! Let's take a look at people in the Bible that God's Word says or implies were wealthy. Matthew 27:57 describes Joseph of Arimathea as rich and also a disciple of Jesus. In Luke 8:3, we learn of Joanna, the wife of Chuza, "Herod's steward, and Susanna, and many others who provided for Him from their substance." Joanna would've been considered wealthy as she was the wife of Herod's steward. I hope you find this as interesting as I did when I thought about the fact that this Herod is a relative of the one who tried to kill Jesus when He was younger, and he slaughtered so many children in that effort to kill Jesus. Yet here, in a roundabout way, his relative is helping to provide for Jesus's needs! I hope this encourages those of you who are working for supervisors you're not comfortable with.

Compare these people to the rich young ruler in Luke 18:18–23:

> Now a certain ruler asked Him, saying, "Good Teacher, what shall I do to inherit eternal life?" So Jesus said to him, "Why do you call Me good? No one is good but One, that is, God. You know the commandments: 'Do not commit adultery,' 'Do not murder,' 'Do not steal,' 'Do not bear false witness,' 'Honor your father and your mother.'" And he said, "All these things I have kept from my youth." So when Jesus heard these things, He said to him, "You still lack one thing. Sell all that you have and distribute to the poor, and you will have treasure in heaven; and come, follow Me." But when he heard this, he became very sorrowful, for he was very rich.

Here, it's obvious that the wealth possessed this ruler. It was not his wealth that kept him from following Christ, but his love and trust in his wealth.

Then there's Zacchaeus in Luke 19:2–9:

> Now behold, there was a man named Zacchaeus who was a chief tax collector, and he was rich. And he sought to see who Jesus was, but could not because of the crowd, for he was of short stature. So he ran ahead and climbed up into a sycamore tree to see Him, for He was going to pass that way. And when Jesus came to the place, He looked up and saw him, and said to him, "Zacchaeus, make haste and come down, for today I must stay at your house." So he made

haste and came down, and received Him joyfully. But when they saw it, they all complained, saying, "He has gone to be a guest with a man who is a sinner." Then Zacchaeus stood and said to the Lord, "Look, Lord, I give half of my goods to the poor; and if I have taken anything from anyone by false accusation, I restore fourfold." And Jesus said to him, "Today salvation has come to this house, because he also is a son of Abraham."

Zacchaeus wanted to see Jesus so much <u>that he ran and climbed up a tree</u>, and his life was blessed from the resulting encounter. But how did he know that the wealth wasn't his since he had only just received Jesus? He didn't even have to be asked. It's obvious that wealth didn't possess him, like it did the rich ruler. Also, since Zacchaeus had wealth and was a chief tax collector, he probably didn't lack wisdom. So I'm going to guess that he never knowingly cheated anyone out of anything. Why would he be so bold as to say that he would restore four times as much if he knew he had cheated someone? Yes, there are some good tax collectors!

Look also at Mary, the mother of John Mark, in Acts 12:12–13: "So, when he had considered this, he came to the house of Mary, the mother of John whose surname was Mark, where many were gathered together praying. And as Peter knocked at the door of the gate, a girl named Rhoda came to answer." This Mary would've been considered wealthy because she had a house big enough to have a large number of people assemble there, as well as a maid (most other Bible versions refer to Rhoda as a servant).

In Acts 16:14–15, we meet Lydia:

Now a certain woman named Lydia heard us. She was a seller of purple from the city of Thyatira, who worshiped God. The Lord opened her heart to heed the things spoken by Paul. And when she and her household were baptized, she begged us, saying, "If you have judged me to be faithful to the Lord, come to my house and stay." So, she persuaded us.

Lydia was a dealer in fabrics. **As a businesswoman**, she must've been a good steward since she worshipped God and had the privilege of Jesus staying at her house.

There are many examples of wealthy Christians in God's Word! What we need to remember is that everything we have belongs to the Lord. We're merely stewards of His grace and benevolence. We are to put our trust in God alone. When you're wealthy, it's very easy to think you have need of nothing, but in fact, everything we have belongs to the Lord. Your wealth is to be used to help others, as the Lord would want you to do. Those who are worldly and wealthy believe they can get or make anything they need, but we are to put our trust in God alone.

Let's look now at what the Bible says about wealth specifically:

> But those who desire to be rich fall into temp-
> tation and a snare, and into many foolish and
> harmful lusts which drown men in destruction
> and perdition. For the love of money is a root
> of all kinds of evil, for which some have strayed
> from the faith in their greediness and pierced
> themselves through with many sorrows. But you,
> O man of God, flee these things and pursue righ-
> teousness, godliness, faith, love, patience, gentle-
> ness. (1 Tim. 6:9–11)

> Command those who are rich in this present
> age not to be haughty, nor to trust in uncertain
> riches but in the living God, who gives us richly
> all things to enjoy. **Let them do good, that they
> be rich in good works, ready to give, willing to
> share, storing up for themselves a good foun-
> dation for the time to come, that they may lay
> hold on eternal life**. (1 Tim. 6:17–19)

The Word doesn't say that you should give away all your money and be poor; it says you should use it wisely. What's more, you can be spiritually rich if your money is used biblically.

> My brethren, do not hold the faith of our Lord Jesus Christ, the Lord of glory, with partiality. For if there should come into your assembly a man with gold rings, in fine apparel, and there should also come in a poor man in filthy clothes, and you pay attention to the one wearing the fine clothes and say to him, "You sit here in a good place," and say to the poor man, "You stand there," or, "Sit here at my footstool," have you not shown partiality among yourselves, and become judges with evil thoughts? Listen, my beloved brethren: Has God not chosen the poor of this world to be rich in faith and heirs of the kingdom which He promised to those who love Him? But you have dishonored the poor man. Do not the rich oppress you and drag you into the courts? Do they not blaspheme that noble name by which you are called? If you really fulfill the **royal law** according to the Scripture, "You shall love your neighbor as yourself," you do well. (James 2:1–8)

> Come now, you rich, weep and howl for your miseries that are coming upon you! Your riches are corrupted, and your garments are moth-eaten. Your gold and silver are corroded, and their corrosion will be a witness against you and will eat your flesh like fire. You have heaped up treasure in the last days. Indeed, the wages of the laborers who mowed your fields, which you kept back by fraud, cry out; and the cries of the reapers have reached the ears of the Lord of Sabbath. You have lived on the earth in pleasure and lux-

ury; you have fattened your hearts as in a day of slaughter. (James 5:1–5)

I know your works, that you are neither cold nor hot. I could wish you were cold or hot. So then, because you are lukewarm, and neither cold nor hot, I will vomit you out of My mouth. Because you say, "I am rich, have become wealthy, and have need of nothing"—and do not know that you are wretched, miserable, poor, blind, and naked. (Rev. 3:15–17)

If you don't use money biblically, *ouch*! What God allows us to have, He expects us to use for His kingdom with His leading and wisdom—whether we be rich or poor.

CHAPTER 5

Seventy Biblical Rewards

A friend of mine once asked me, "If it's not God's, then whose is it?" He also added, "If we don't give to God's work, Satan has the right to get it, and he'll take much more than God is asking for." God blesses when we give, as He has asked us to do.

In an effort to help you track these rewards in your own Bible, I started with Matthew and worked my way through by book. reminder I copied and pasted NKJV. Let's look now at the rewards we get for following God's Word in our lives.

> You have heard that it was said, "You shall love
> your neighbor and hate your enemy." But I say
> to you, love your enemies, bless those who curse
> you, do good to those who hate you, and pray for
> those who spitefully use you and persecute you,
> that you may be **sons of your Father** in heaven
> **[Reward #1]**; for He makes His sun rise on the
> evil and on the good, and sends rain on the just
> and on the unjust. For if you love those who love
> you, what reward have you? Do not even the tax
> collectors do the same? And if you greet your
> brethren only, what do you do more than others?
> Do not even the tax collectors do so? Therefore,
> **you shall be perfect** **[Reward #2]**, just as your

Father in heaven is perfect. (Matt. 5:43–48; also
Luke 6:30–36)

When we use our time to love, pray for, and do good to our
enemies, the blessing is that we are confirming our sonship with the
Father. His own Son endured no less on His journey to the grave;
how much less should we be like Christ? And as Christ rose from the
grave, victorious over sin and death, so shall you!

Did you notice that through the correct use of your time
and money, you can reach perfection? Wow, what a blessing! The
word *perfection* in this verse means "completion" or "moral upright-
ness." God wants us to be complete and morally upright in Him.
Remember, David referred to this "perfection": "Mark the perfect
man and behold the upright: for the end of that man is peace" (Ps.
37:37, KJV).

This perfection doesn't mean you'll never fail; it means that
you have achieved everything that God wants from you in that
moment. We should strive to live every moment for Him! The
only thing that could stop us from achieving completeness is the
number-one tool that Satan uses: the *self*. Think about it: When it
comes to sharing, our time and money seem to be the hardest areas
for us to acknowledge that we are just God's stewards. If you boil
down your resistance to tithing, giving, and serving, you'll discover
your own self-interest, self-ownership, and lack of *true* stewardship.
We own nothing!

With the correct use of money, we can get rid of self-interest—
Satan's number-one tool against us. If the Lord has our money, He
almost assuredly has the rest of us. Some people resist the idea of
selflessness; after all, if one is taking care of their body, aren't they also
only taking care of their *self*? No! It's not *our* bodies. If we are truly
the Lord's, we're merely the stewards of our bodies. Therefore, taking
care of your body is not an act of self-interest. You are taking care
of His property. It *would* be self-interest if all your time and money
were spent on taking care of your body for a vain reason or in an
obsessive way that does not help others. When we have time and
money invested in helping others, <u>we tend to care for others and have</u>

a healthy sense of ourselves. **Plus, it forces us to think about Jesus more since we are doing it for Him**.

> Take heed that you do not do your charitable deeds before men, to be seen by them. Otherwise you have no reward from your Father in heaven. Therefore, when you do a charitable deed, do not sound a trumpet before you as the hypocrites do in the synagogues and in the streets, that they may have glory from men. Assuredly, I say to you, they have their reward. But when you do a charitable deed, do not let your left hand know what your right hand is doing, that your charitable deed may be in secret; and your Father who sees in secret **will Himself reward you openly [Reward #3]**. (Matt. 6:1–4)

A charitable deed is an act of kindness that is done to help others while seeking nothing in return, and it, of course, takes time or money. I look back at times when I helped others and was disappointed because I didn't even get a thank-you. Now, when I can, I try to find ways to help others anonymously. Then it doesn't bother me if I'm not thanked; I would rather have my heavenly Father reward me anyway!

> Do not lay up for yourselves treasures on earth, where moth and rust destroy and where thieves break in and steal; but lay up for yourselves treasures in heaven, where neither moth nor rust destroys and where thieves do not break in and steal. **For where your treasure is, there your heart will be also [Reward #4]**. (Matt. 6:19–21; also Luke 12:33–34)

Can you imagine the protection our hearts could receive if we were to store our treasures in heaven? Why can't it be our real heart!

It is one of the treasures that God gave me. About fifteen years ago, I had a triple bypass. I was going to work on a Wednesday morning, and before I arrived at my office, I had a pain in the top of my chest, underneath my chin. It wasn't a location that I had ever heard could be an indication of a heart problem. I look back now and believe it was the Holy Spirit who prompted me to go into the emergency room. When I walked in, the nurse asked me what was wrong, and I pointed to where the pain was. She said it probably wasn't anything serious. When she took hold of my arm to take my blood pressure, she asked if my skin was normally clammy, and as soon as I said no, she decided to do some testing. Within three or four hours, they knew there was something really wrong: One of my veins was 100 percent blocked. Another was 85 percent blocked, and a third was 40 percent blocked. It was serious enough that they sent me by ambulance to a different hospital that afternoon, where they scheduled a triple bypass for Friday morning. Now, before you ask how God was protecting my heart, I want to tell you that there was no heart attack or stroke that sent me to the hospital. From what I understand, it is quite common to find a vein problem <u>after</u> a heart attack or stroke.

Think about this: If you use up all your assets during your life here on yourself, what treasures will you have for your eternity in heaven?

> Therefore, do not worry, saying, "What shall we <u>eat</u>?" or "What shall we <u>drink</u>?" or "What shall we <u>wear</u>?" For after all these things the Gentiles seek. For your heavenly Father knows that you need all these things. But seek first the kingdom of God and His righteousness, **all these things shall be added to you [Reward #5]**. (Matt 6:31–33, also Matt. 10:9–10)

Wow, what a blessing reward number 5 is! Seeking the kingdom of God involves worship and ministry, and ministry always involves either time or money—or both. Remember that the time spent on a work is as valuable as money. So again, time is money. Even if we are not paid in money, we are paid with a replacement of it. Some of my ancestors even used beads, blankets, and horses when they made exchanges. To them, they were the same as money. So, whether you spend time or money, you are learning to trust the Lord more and further His kingdom.

> Not everyone who says to Me, "Lord, Lord," shall **enter the kingdom of heaven [Reward #6]**, **but he who does the will of My Father in heaven**. (Matt. 7:21)

And of course, "the will of the Father" is that we first accept His grace and forgiveness for our salvation **and** then spread the gospel and serve others. The importance of the above passage should not be overlooked. There are people who think they will enter the kingdom of heaven but will not, as this passage clearly states. Please pray for the discernment to be able to judge yourself. Have you accepted Christ's atonement for your sins? Are you doing the will of the Father?

> Therefore whoever hears these sayings of Mine, **and does them, I will liken him to a wise man** [**Reward #7**] who built his house on the rock: and the rain descended, the floods came, and the winds blew and beat on that house; and it did not fall, for it was **founded on the rock** [**Reward #8**]. (Matt. 7:24–25, also Luke 6:46–49)

Is there anyone who doesn't want Jesus to consider them wise? I surely don't want to be considered a stupid person by Him. And guess what? I don't believe there's any middle ground. You're either a wise man or a foolish one. A wise man or woman may not know everything but would continually seek knowledge. Building my house upon the Rock (Jesus) has certainly been the best decision I have ever made.

Reward #9

> Now when Jesus had come into Peter's house,
> He saw his wife's mother lying sick with a fever.
> So He touched her hand, and the fever left her.
> And she arose and served them. When evening
> had come, they brought to Him many who were
> demon-possessed. And He cast out the spir-
> its with a word, and **healed all who were sick**
> **[Reward #9]**, that it might be fulfilled which
> was spoken by Isaiah the prophet, saying: "He
> Himself took our infirmities and bore our sick-
> nesses." (Matt. 8:14–17; see also Mark 1:29–34
> and Luke 4:38–41)

Jesus was welcomed into Peter's house. Mark 1:33 says, "And the whole city was gathered together at the door." If Peter had not received Jesus into his house because his cupboards were bare or because he didn't want to spend his time, look at the blessings he would've missed out on. His mother-in-law was healed. Can you imagine how long his house was remembered by the whole city as the place where Jesus healed many? How many times do you suppose he was thanked for allowing the people to gather at his door to receive healing? When we invite God into our lives, the reward is that He does His work through us!

> And when He had called his twelve disciples to
> Him, He gave them power over unclean spirits,
> **to cast them out** [Reward #10], and **to heal**
> **all kinds of sickness and all kinds of disease**
> [Reward #11]. (Matt. 10:1)

Again, God uses those who give their lives to Him. The reward is that He empowers us to further His kingdom. We don't need to have special gifts or talents because He uses all who come to Him.

> Now whatever city or town you enter, inquire who in it is worthy, and stay there till you go out. And when you go into a household, greet it. If the **household is worthy** [**Reward #12**], let your **peace come upon it** [**Reward #13**]. But if it is not worthy, let your peace return to you. And whoever will not receive you nor hear your words, when you depart from that house or city, shake off the dust from your feet. Assuredly, I say to you, it will be more tolerable for the land of Sodom and Gomorrah, in the Day of Judgment, than for that city! (Matt. 10:11–15)

I'm sure there isn't anyone out there who would not want more peace in his or her household. Our household could be considered *worthy* by the Lord if we spend time and money to help the worker. And, of course, the disciple's peace is the Lord's peace. I'm sure we all want more of His peace!

Who wouldn't want a disciple to stay in his or her house—one with the power and authority over all demons and who can cure diseases and heal the sick? I would want one to stay at my house 24 hours a day, 365 days a year!

> And he who does not take his cross and follow after Me is not **worthy of Me** [**Reward #14**]. He who finds his life will lose it, and he who loses his life for My sake **will find it** [**Reward #15**]. He who receives you receives Me, and he who receives Me **receives Him who sent Me** [**Reward #16**]. (Matt. 10:38–40; also Mark 9:41 and Luke 9:48, 14:26–27)

Okay, let's stop right here. There's no sense in going any further. There can be no greater rewards than the ones in verses fourteen through sixteen. If this doesn't convince you that spending time and money on this is worth it, nothing will. Since the joy of the Lord is my strength, and He said it is more blessed to give than to receive, I want to be in that position where He can continue to give me His blessing.

> He who receives a prophet in the name of a prophet shall **receive a prophet's reward** [**Reward #17**]. And he who receives a righteous man in the name of a righteous man shall **receive a righteous man's reward** [**Reward #18**]. And whoever gives one of these little ones only a cup of cold water in the name of a disciple, assuredly, I say to you, he shall by no means lose his reward. (Matt. 10:41–42)

It's obvious in the above verse that the prophet and the righteous man are "these little ones." When we receive a true prophet, we receive Jesus. We therefore receive the Father, and thereby we receive a prophet's reward. When we receive a righteous man, we receive a righteous man's reward.

> Take My yoke upon you and learn from Me, for I am gentle and lowly in heart, and you will find **rest for your souls** [**Reward #19**]. For My yoke is easy and My burden is light. (Matt. 11:29–30)

His yoke is for us to follow His example of being a servant. We don't want to be lazy servants because we know He wasn't lazy. Rest for our souls? As I look back on my life, I realize that the more trust I had put in the Lord—giving Him the opportunity to prove His love for me (which He desires to do for everyone), the more refreshed I felt. Think of the rest that you have when you're not worrying. The more trust you put in the Lord, the less you worry. Of course, the hardest thing to turn over to the Lord is our use of money and time. I don't know about you, but the more I'm reminded that it's not *my* life (it's His life), the better I feel. The only time I worry is when I forget that it's His life. If it's His life, *why* do I need to worry?

The bottom line is that I either trust Jesus or I don't, especially when it comes to Him supplying my needs. To help remind me of this, every time I open my billfold, I see a note taped in there that says, A life lived for others is a life worth living. I know there have been many times when I opened my billfold to use my debit or credit card to buy something and that note reminded me to think about whether I really needed that purchase. All too often I didn't! Seeing that note helped me spend much less money on myself. **It has been the best budget tool I've ever used**. Come to think of it, I don't recall any heavenly rewards for money spent on myself, except for the things that teach me to be a better servant, as the living example, Jesus, showed us.

> Therefore, hear the parable of the sower: when anyone hears the word of the kingdom, and does not understand it, then the wicked one comes and snatches away what was sown in his heart. This is he who received seed by the wayside. But he who received the seed on stony places, this is he who hears the word and immediately receives it with joy; yet he has no root in himself, but endures only for a while. For when tribulation or persecution arises because of the word, immediately he stumbles. Now he who received seed among the thorns is he who hears the word, and the cares of this world and the deceitfulness of riches choke the word, and he becomes unfruitful. But he who received seed on the good ground is he who hears the word and understands it, **who indeed bears** fruit and produces: **some a hundredfold, some sixty, some thirty [Reward #20]**." (Matt. 13:18–23; also Mark 4:13–20; Luke 8:11–15)

Good ground receives the fertilizer of the Word. The more knowledge of the Word we have, the stronger our roots are. As a securities and life-insurance professional, I would say that ninety-nine out of a hundred people who try to get a return of over two times in a year (let alone thirty times or more on their investment) will lose it all. But guess what? With the Lord, all things are possible. When you're working for Him, the minimum return could be one hundred times the investment!

Remember the young lad who gave his five loaves and two fish to the Lord. We know that when the Lord was looking up to heaven, He was first giving them to God. The Bible says that Christ took them and fed over five thousand men, plus whatever number of women and children were there. There were twelve full baskets left over. What if the person who had the bread and fish had decided that he would eat them himself or only share with his friends? He might have been able to feed ten to fifteen at the very most instead of the more than five thousand who were fed that day.

> Now behold, one came and said to Him, "Good teacher, what good thing shall I do that I may have eternal life?" So He said to him, "Why do you call Me good? No one is good but One, that is, God. But if you want to enter into life, keep the commandments." He said to Him, "Which ones?" Jesus said, "'You shall not murder,' 'You shall not commit adultery,' 'You shall not steal,' 'You shall not bear false witness,' 'Honor your father and your mother,' and, 'You shall love your neighbor as yourself.'" The young man said to Him, "All these things I have kept from my youth. What do I still lack?" Jesus said to him, **"If you want to be perfect** [Reward #2 again], go, sell what you have and give to the poor, and **you will have treasure in heaven** [Reward #21]; and come, follow Me." But when the young man heard that saying, he went away sorrowful, for he had great possessions. (Matt. 19:16–22; also Mark 10:17–22 and Luke 18:18–23)

As far as I'm concerned, the rich man in this story was really a very poor man. He was only satisfied with earthly pleasures. Try to imagine how much greater the treasures in heaven are. **Did you notice that giving and being perfect are tied together again**? Also, why would this rich young ruler be asked to sell all he had when the chief tax collector, Zacchaeus (Luke 19:8), only gave half of his wealth (plus four times anything he had taken falsely from anyone)? Think about this: Being a chief tax collector, he probably wasn't without wisdom when he made the statement about giving four times what he had wrongfully taken. I believe he knew he hadn't taken anything by false means (i.e., by saying that someone owed more taxes than he or she really did). Most of us know if we have stolen from someone. As for the rich young ruler, if he had really kept the Ten Commandments, he would've known he was supposed to help the poor. So, it probably would not have made a difference if he were asked to give just a part of what he had instead of all. His self-interest was too great. His wealth possessed him (a curse). Yet Zacchaeus, whom the crowd accused of being a sinner, had not even been asked to give anything. Through his voluntary action, salvation came to his house. The Amplified Bible says that salvation came to **all** the members of that household (a reward).

> And everyone who has left houses or brothers or sisters or father or mother or wife or children or lands, for My name's sake, shall receive a hundredfold [**Reward #20** again], and **inherit eternal life** [**Reward #22**]. (Matt. 19:29; also Mark 10:30)

Again, God returns on your investment for Him!

> For the kingdom of heaven is like a man traveling to a far country, who called his own servants and delivered his goods to them. And to one he gave five talents, to another two, and to another one, to each according to his own ability. And

immediately he went on a journey. Then he who had received the five talents went and traded with them, and made another five talents. And likewise he who had received two gained two more also. But he who had received one went and dug in the ground, and hid his lord's money. After a long time the lord of those servants came and settled accounts with them. So he who had received five talents came and brought five other talents, saying, "Lord, you delivered to me five talents; look, I have gained five more talents besides them." His lord said to him, **<u>Well done, good and faithful servant</u>** [**Reward #23**]; you were faithful over a few things, I will make you ruler over many things. **<u>Enter into the joy of your lord</u>** [**Reward #24**]." He also who had received two talents came and said, "Lord, you delivered to me two talents; look, I have gained two more talents besides them." His lord said to him, "<u>Well done, good and faithful servant</u> [**Reward #23** again]; you have been faithful over a few things, I will make you ruler over many things. <u>Enter into the joy of your lord</u> [**Reward #24** again]." Then he who had received the one talent came and said, "Lord, I knew you to be a hard man, reaping where you have not sown, and gathering where you have not scattered seed. And I was afraid, and went and hid your talent in the ground. Look, there you have what is yours." But his lord answered and said to him, "You wicked and lazy servant, you knew that I reap where I have not sown and gather where I have not scattered seed." (Matt. 25:14–26; also Luke 19:11–27)

The above scripture shows us that the Lord knows what we are capable of. And even though in the parable, He knew the third servant would not work, He gave him an opportunity anyway. But guess what? Even if we were like the third servant in our past, God is always ready to forgive and offer another chance. Hebrews 13:5 says, "He himself has said, 'I will never leave you nor forsake you.'" The first two servants went to work with what they were given and received a hundredfold return. The third one didn't work, and the Lord called him a wicked and lazy servant. I pray that we will never be called wicked and lazy by the Lord.

> For to everyone who has, more will be given, and he will **have abundance** [**Reward #25**]; but from him who does not have, even what he has will be taken away. (Matt. 25:29)

> And He will set the sheep on His right hand, but the goats on the left. Then the King will say to those on His right hand, "**Come, you blessed of My Father** [**Reward #26**], inherit the kingdom [**Reward #6** again] prepared for you from the foundation of the world: for I was hungry and you gave Me food; I was thirsty and you gave Me drink; I was a stranger and you took Me in; I was naked and you clothed Me; I was sick and you visited Me; I was in prison and you came to Me." Then the righteous will answer Him, saying, "Lord, when did we see You hungry and feed You, or thirsty and give You drink? When did we see You a stranger and take You in, or naked and clothe You? Or when did we see You sick, or in prison, and come to You?" And the King will answer and say to them, "Assuredly, I say to you, inasmuch as you did it to one of the least of these My brethren, **you did it to Me** [**Reward #27**]." (Matt. 25:33–40)

In the above scripture, we are reminded of how important it is for us to serve others, thereby serving our Father.

And these will go away into everlasting punishment, but <u>the righteous into eternal life</u> [**Reward #6** again]. (Matt. 25:46)

And when Jesus was in Bethany at the house of Simon the leper, a woman came to Him having an alabaster flask of very costly fragrant oil [worth approximately $6,000 today], and she poured it on His head as He sat at the table. But when His disciples saw it, they were indignant, saying, "Why this waste? For this fragrant oil might have been sold for much and given to the poor." But when Jesus was aware of it, He said to them, "Why do you trouble the woman? For she has done a good work for Me. For you have the poor with you always, but Me you do not have always. For in pouring this fragrant oil on My body, she did it for My burial. Assuredly, I say to you, wherever this gospel is preached in the whole world, what this woman has done will also be told **as a memorial to her** [**Reward #28**]." (Matt. 26:6–13; also Mark 14:3–9; Luke 7:36–50; John 12:1–8)

Food for thought: It appears to me that it really had not yet sunk into the disciples that He was going to lay his life down for all, yet this woman seemed to know. It reminds me of the saying "The Holy Spirit moves in mysterious ways"—mysterious to us, but, of course, not to the Father.

In Luke 7:1–10, we read of a centurion with a beloved servant who was dying of an unnamed illness. When he heard about Jesus, he sent elders of the Jews to Him, pleading for Him to come heal his servant. Jesus went with them to the centurion's house, but the centurion sent friends to Him, saying, "Lord, do not trouble Yourself, for I am not worthy that You should enter under my roof. Therefore I did not even think myself worthy to come to You. But say the word, and my servant will be healed. For I also am a man placed under authority, having soldiers under me. And I say to one, 'Go,' and he goes; and to another, 'Come,' and he comes; and to my servant, 'Do this,' and he does it." At these words, Jesus marveled and said to the crowd following Him, "I say to you, I have not found such great faith, not even in Israel!" And immediately the servant was healed!

A centurion was commonly thought to have had a hundred to a thousand men working under him. Can you imagine what it would be like to be a mere servant to a man who cared so much about you? He was a Roman pleading with Jesus to heal his servant. His friends said the centurion deserved to have his servant healed because he loved the Jewish nation and had built them a synagogue. What a steward he must've been. There probably aren't too many Christians who would build a synagogue. He received a healing (a blessing) for someone who was dear to him.

This man with earthly authority knew that Jesus's authority was so great that Jesus didn't even have to enter his house to heal his servant. We do know that Christ healed his servant (a blessing). The centurion was representing Rome, his government. What a great country this could be if our leaders looked after the people like he did. Leaders, too, are stewards.

> Then the Lord said to him, "Now you Pharisees make the outside of the cup and dish clean, but your inward part is full of greed and wickedness. Foolish ones! Did not He who made the outside make the inside also? **But rather give alms of such things as you have**; then **indeed all things are clean to you** [Reward #29]. (Luke 11:39–41)

> Woe to you lawyers! For you have **taken away the key of knowledge** [Reward #30]. You did not enter in yourselves, and those who were entering in you hindered. (Luke 11:52)

Alms are acts or deeds of mercy. Like the Pharisees, we all know how to make the outside clean, but sometimes we struggle with the inside. The Word says that all things are clean to us if we commit acts or deeds of mercy. Wow! I don't believe I'm oversimplifying it; you know that Jesus's life was focused on alms (helping others). Is not our goal to become more like Jesus?

I have read verse fifty-two many times, and it never truly sank in until now that the key of knowledge is in alms. By reason of use! I look back on how many times I asked God for wisdom and knowledge, not realizing that the key that would give me access to knowledge was in alms. Start helping others, and you will gain knowledge.

> Do not fear, little flock, for it is **your Father's good pleasure** [Reward #31] <u>to give you the kingdom</u> [Reward #6 again]. Sell what you have and give alms; provide yourselves money bags which do not grow old, a treasure in the heavens that does not fail, where no thief approaches nor moth destroys. For where your treasure is, there your heart will be also. (Luke 12:32–34)

If you possess it (it's yours, not God's), it actually possess you, as it did the rich young ruler who could not let go (Matt. 19:16; Mark 10:17; Luke 18:18). His self was holding him back. I look back and remember two things I had that really had me because I had so much pride and joy in their being mine. One was a heavy, solid, eighteen-karat gold necklace. The other was a large, beautiful diamond ring. I justified keeping them much longer than I should have by saying that I could never get what I had paid for them if I sold them. Even though that turned out to be true, <u>I gained so much more when</u> I did finally get rid of them. The unspeakable joy that came over me at that time, the release I felt—I'll never get over it. No pun intended, but it really was like a weight coming off me.

You may wonder, "How can I provide for myself if I'm giving things away?" In God's eyes, He sees a steward that He can use. He gives more when you give more. Giving is like the power in a car. We know the car can't start unless it has power. We don't really start receiving until we give, which turns the power on. If your treasure is in heaven, your heart is there also. What a blessing! And in Matthew 6:19, the curse is the treasures stored here on earth. These can be lost and corrupted **and remain here when we die.**

> Then He also said to him who invited Him, "When you give a dinner or a supper, do not ask your friends, your brothers, your relatives, nor rich neighbors, lest they also invite you back, and you be repaid. But when you give a feast, invite the poor, the maimed, the lame, the blind. And you will be blessed, because they cannot repay you; for **you shall be repaid** [**Reward #32**] at the resurrection of the just." (Luke 14:12–14)

> He who is faithful in the least is faithful also in much; and he who is unjust in what is least is unjust also in much. Therefore, if you have not been faithful in the unrighteous mammon, who will commit to your trust **the true riches** [**Reward #33**]? And if you have not been faithful in what is another man's, who will give you **what is your own** [**Reward #34**]? No servant can serve two masters; for either he will hate the one and love the other, or else he will be loyal to the one and despise the other. You cannot serve God and mammon. (Luke 16:10–13)

Even though we can't serve God and mammon, we can, without a shadow of doubt, use mammon to serve God. If you look at it through the world's eyes, you may believe you have very little to give. In God's eyes, if you are a faithful steward, He can trust you with much more (a blessing). If you are unjust or unfaithful, why would He trust you with true riches? As Jesus said, you can only serve one master. You can serve the self through earthly wealth (mammon), or you can serve God.

Now behold, there was a man named Zacchaeus who was a chief tax collector, and he was rich. And he sought to see who Jesus was, but could not because of the crowd, for he was of short stature. So he ran ahead and climbed up into a sycamore tree to see Him, for He was going to pass that way. And when Jesus came to the place, He looked up and saw him, and said to him, "Zacchaeus, make haste and come down, for today I must stay at your house." So he made haste and came down, and received Him joyfully. But when they saw it, they all complained, saying, "He has gone to be a guest with a man who is a sinner." Then Zacchaeus stood and said to the Lord, "Look, Lord, I give half of my goods to the poor; and if I have taken anything from anyone by false accusation, I restore fourfold." And Jesus said to him, "Today **salvation has come to this house** [Reward #35], because he also is a son of Abraham; for the Son of Man has come to seek and to save that which was lost." (Luke 19:2–10)

At Joppa there was a certain disciple named Tabitha, which is translated Dorcas. This woman was full of good works and charitable deeds which she did. But it happened in those days that she became sick and died. When they had washed her, they laid her in an upper room. And since Lydda was near Joppa, and the disciples had heard that Peter was there, they sent two men to him, imploring him not to delay in coming to them. Then Peter arose and went with them. When he had come, they brought him to the upper room. And all the widows stood by him weeping, showing the tunics and garments which Dorcas had made while she was with them. But Peter put them all out and knelt down and prayed. And turning to the body he said, "Tabitha, arise." And she opened her eyes, and when she saw Peter she sat up. Then he gave her his hand and lifted her up; and when he had called the saints and widows, **he presented her alive** [**Reward #36**]. And it became known throughout all Joppa, and **many believed on the Lord** [**Reward #37**]. (Acts 9:36–42)

Tabitha's work of making tunics and garments for the people around her caused the people to love her so much that they went out of their way (it was approximately a twenty-mile round trip) to implore the apostle Peter to come see her and bring her back to life. The Word says that many believed on the Lord because of her.

And they said, "Cornelius the centurion, a just man, one who fears God and has a good reputation among all the nation of the Jews, **was divinely instructed by a holy angel** [**Reward #38**] to summon you to his house, and to hear words from you." Then he invited them in and lodged them. On the next day Peter went away with them, and some brethren from Joppa accompanied him. And the following day they entered Caesarea. Now Cornelius was waiting for them, and had called together his relatives and close friends. As Peter was coming in, Cornelius met him and fell down at his feet and worshiped him. But Peter lifted him up, saying, "Stand up; I myself am also a man." And as he talked with him, he went in and found many who had come together. Then he said to them, "You know how unlawful it is for a Jewish man to keep company with or go to one of another nation. But God has shown me that I should not call any man common or unclean. Therefore I came without objection as soon as I was sent for. I ask, then, for what reason have you sent for me?" So Cornelius said, "Four days ago I was fasting until this hour; and at the ninth hour I prayed in my house, and behold, a man stood before me in bright clothing, and said, 'Cornelius, your prayer has been heard, and your alms are **remembered in the sight of God** [**Reward #39**]. Send therefore to Joppa and call Simon here, whose surname is Peter. He is lodging in the house of Simon, a tanner, by the sea. When he comes, he will speak to you.' So I sent to you immediately, and you have done well to come. Now therefore, we are all present before God, to hear all the things commanded you by God." (Acts 10:22–33)

Can you imagine the experience Cornelius had? A man in bright clothing stood before him and told him that his prayers and alms were remembered in the sight of God. He knew this was a supernatural experience. This is another great example of what happens when alms are involved.

While Peter was still speaking these words, **the Holy Spirit fell upon all those who heard** [**Reward #40**] the word. And those of the circumcision who believed were astonished, as many as came with Peter, because the gift of the Holy Spirit had been poured out on the Gentiles also. For they heard them speak with tongues and magnify God. Then Peter answered, "Can anyone forbid water, that these should not be baptized who have received the Holy Spirit just as we have?" And he commanded them to be baptized in the name of the Lord. (Acts 10:44–48)

What joy Cornelius must have felt when his relatives and close friends had the Holy Spirit fall upon them and were baptized in the name of the Lord! And what joy for Peter also! God really showed him that He shows no partiality. And **it all started because of his use of time and money.**

> So now, brethren, I commend you to God and to the word of His grace, which is able to build you up and give you an inheritance among all those who are sanctified. I have coveted no one's silver or gold or apparel. Yes, you yourselves know that these hands have provided for my necessities, and for those who were with me. I have shown you in every way, by laboring like this, that you must support the weak. And remember the words of the Lord Jesus, that He said, **"It is more blessed to give than to receive"** [**Reward #41**]. (Acts 20:32–35)

We must support the weak. And even though we are blessed when we receive, we are <u>more blessed</u> when we give.

> Moreover, brethren, we make known to you the **grace of God bestowed** [**Reward #42**] on the churches of Macedonia: that in a great trial of affliction the **abundance of their joy** [**Reward #43**] and their deep poverty abounded in the riches of their liberality. For I bear witness that according to their ability, yes, and beyond their ability, they were freely willing, imploring us with much urgency that we would receive the gift and the fellowship of the ministering to the saints. And not only as we had hoped, but they first gave themselves to the Lord, and then to us by the will of God. So we urged Titus, that as he had begun, so he would also complete this

grace in you as well. But as you abound in everything—in faith, in speech, in knowledge, in all
diligence, and in your love for us—see that you
abound in this grace also. I speak not by commandment, but I am testing the sincerity of your
love by the diligence of others. For you know the
grace of our Lord Jesus Christ, that though He
was rich, yet for your sakes He became poor, that
you through His poverty might become rich.
And in this I give advice: **it is to your advantage** [**Reward #44**] not only to be doing what
you began and were desiring to do a year ago;
but now you also must complete the doing of it;
that as there was a readiness to desire it, so there
also may be a completion out of what you have.
For if there is first a willing mind, it is accepted
according to what one has, and not according to
what he does not have. For I do not mean that
others should be eased and you burdened; but by
an equality, that now at this time your abundance
may supply their lack, that their abundance also
may supply your lack—that there may be equality. (2 Cor. 8:1–14)

Verse twelve tells us that if there is first a willing mind, it makes
no difference how little you may have. Verse two says that we can
receive joy even in our deep poverty! I believe the reason we can
receive joy in our deep poverty is because we are still giving, thereby
proving we trust and love the Lord.

But this I say: He who sows sparingly will also
reap sparingly, and he who sows bountifully will
also reap bountifully. So, let each one give as he
purposes in his heart, not grudgingly or of neces-
sity; for God loves a cheerful giver. And God is
able to make all grace abound toward you, that

you, always having all **sufficiency in all things** [**Reward #45**], may have an abundance for every good work [**Reward #26** again]. As it is written: "He has dispersed abroad, He has given to the poor; His righteousness endures forever." Now may He who supplies seed to the sower, and bread for food, supply and multiply the seed you have sown [**Reward #20** again] and **increase the fruits of your righteousness** [**Reward #46**], while you are enriched in everything for all liberality, which causes thanksgiving through us to God. For the administration of this service not only supplies the needs of the saints, but also is abounding through many thanksgivings to God [**Reward #47**] while, through the proof of this ministry, they glorify God for the obedience of your confession to the gospel of Christ, and for your liberal sharing with them and all men, and **by their prayer for you** [**Reward #48**], who long for you because of **the exceeding grace of God in you** [**Reward #49**]. Thanks be to God for His indescribable gift! (2 Cor. 9:6–15)

If you start giving, you will begin to trust more in the Lord. If you don't give, you're saying that you don't trust the Lord. Even if you don't have money, remember that time is money if the time is used wisely. Ask your pastor if there is someone who needs help in your church—for example, someone may be ill and need help with mowing their lawn or cleaning their house. If you have a voice, why not smile at the next person you meet and tell them, "Jesus loves you." Can you imagine the blessing the Lord will give you if a person receives Jesus as their Lord because of your small effort? And what if they don't receive the Lord? Your effort will still be rewarded. But sooner or later, someone will respond. If you truly want to be blessed, even when you don't have assets or money to give, you can find a way to **help someone with your time**. Galatians 6:4–5 says,

"But let each one examine his own work, and then he will have rejoicing in himself alone, and not in another. For each one shall bear his own load." Think about how good you feel when you finish a project that you started, especially if it's something you didn't think you could do. You'll be giving all the glory to the Lord for his helping you!

> Not that I have already attained, or am already perfected; but I press on [keep going], that I may lay hold of that for which Christ Jesus has also laid hold of me. Brethren, I do not count myself to have apprehended; but one thing I do, forgetting those things which are behind and reaching forward to those things which are ahead, I press toward the goal for the prize of the **upward call of God** [**Reward #50**] in Christ Jesus. Therefore, let us, as many as are mature, have this mind; and if in anything you think otherwise, God will reveal even this to you. Nevertheless, to the degree that we have already attained, let us walk by the same rule, let us be of the same mind. (Phil. 3:12–16)

Even if I tried, I probably couldn't count the number of times that this scripture saved me when Satan reminded me of my past in an effort to try to defeat me. I know that God *totally* forgets my sins—even if *I* don't forget—because this scripture says so. I do know that I am forgiven when I ask for forgiveness.

> And let our people also learn to maintain good works, to meet urgent needs, **that they may not be unfruitful** [**Reward #51**]. (Titus 3:14)

> But do not forget to do good and to share, for with such sacrifices **God is well pleased** [**Reward #52**]. (Heb. 13:16)

But **be doers of the word**, and <u>**not hearers only, deceiving yourselves**</u>. For if anyone is a hearer of the word and not a doer, he is like a man observing his natural face in a mirror; for he observes himself, goes away, and immediately forgets what kind of man he was. But he who looks into the perfect law of liberty and continues in it and is not a forgetful hearer but a doer of the work, this one will be <u>**blessed in what he does**</u> **[Reward #53].** If anyone among you thinks he is religious and does not bridle his tongue but deceives his own heart, this one's religion is useless. Pure and undefiled religion before God and the Father is this: to visit orphans and widows in their trouble, and to keep oneself unspotted from the world. (James 1:22–27)

Remember, the Scriptures say we are to help those who cannot return the favor; if we do so, God will openly reward us.

So speak and so do as those who will be judged by the law of liberty. For judgment is without mercy to the one who has shown no mercy. Mercy triumphs over judgment. What does it profit, my brethren, if someone says he has faith but does not have works? Can faith save him? If a brother or sister is naked and destitute of daily food, and one of you says to them, "Depart in peace, be warmed and filled," but you do not give them the things which are needed for the body, what does it profit? Thus also faith by itself, if it does not have works, is dead. But someone will say, "You have faith, and I have works." Show me your faith without your works, and I will show you my faith by my works. You believe that there is one God. You do well. Even the demons believe—and tremble! But do you want to know, O foolish man, that faith without works is dead? Was not Abraham our father justified by works when he offered Isaac his son on the altar? Do you see that <u>faith was working together with his works</u>, and **by works faith was made perfect** [**Reward #54**]? And the Scripture was fulfilled which says, "Abraham believed God, and it was accounted to him for righteousness." And he was **called the friend of God** [**Reward #55**]. You see then that <u>a man is justified by works</u> [**Reward #56**], and **not by faith only**. Likewise, was not Rahab the harlot also justified by works when she received the messengers and sent them out another way? For as the body without the spirit is dead, so faith without works is dead also. (James 2:12–26)

I think it's pretty easy to understand that Abraham was justified by works, but so was Rahab the harlot. This is really amazing and should give us all hope in our works. We're no better than Rahab, but faith was given to her so that she could do good works. Verse twenty-two says that by works, faith is made perfect (i.e., complete).

By this we **know love** [**Reward #57**], because He laid down His life for us. And we also ought to lay down our lives for the brethren. But whoever has this world's goods, and sees his brother in need, and shuts up his heart from him, how does the love of God abide in him? My little children, let us not love in word or with tongue, but in deed and truth. And by this we **know that we are of the truth** [**Reward #58**] and shall **assure our hearts before Him** [**Reward #59**]. For if our heart condemns us, God is greater than our heart, and knows all things. Beloved, if our heart does not condemn us, we **have confidence toward God**. [**Reward #60**]. And **whatever we ask, we receive from Him** [**Reward #61**] **because** we keep His commandments and do those things that are pleasing in His sight [**Reward #52** again]. And this is His commandment: that we should believe on the name of His Son Jesus Christ and love one another, as He gave us commandment. Now he who keeps His commandments **abides in Him** [**Reward #62**], and **He in him** [**Reward #63**]. And by this we know that He abides in us, by the Spirit whom He has given us. (1 John 3:16–24)

If we want to know or experience love, we need to live for others. Ultimately, I do not believe there is anyone who does not—deep down—want to experience love. The sooner you start helping others, the sooner you will experience it.

By our work, we assure our hearts before God, and this gives us confidence toward God since we know we're pleasing Him. Who in their right mind would not want to please God? I can't think of a greater joy than to know that I am pleasing God.

Beloved, I pray that you may prosper in all things and be in health, just as your soul prospers. For I rejoiced greatly when brethren came and testified of the truth that is in you, just as you walk in the truth. **I have no greater joy** [**Reward #64**] than to hear that my children walk in truth. Beloved, you do faithfully whatever you do for the brethren and for strangers, who have borne **witness of your love before the church** [**Reward #65**]. If you send them forward on their journey in a manner worthy of God, **you will do well** [**Reward #66**], because they went forth for His name's sake, taking nothing from the Gentiles.

We therefore ought to receive such, that we may become fellow workers for the truth. I wrote to the church, but Diotrephes, who loves to have the preeminence among them, does not receive us. Therefore, if I come, I will call to mind his deeds which he does, prating against us with malicious words. And not content with that, he himself does not receive the brethren, and forbids those who wish to, putting them out of the church. Beloved, do not imitate what is evil, but what is good. He **who does good is of God** [**Reward #67**], but he who does evil has not seen God. (3 John 2–11)

"And behold, I am coming quickly, and My reward is with Me [**Reward #68**] to give to every one according to his work. I am the Alpha and the Omega, the Beginning and the End, the First and the Last." Blessed [**Reward #27** again] are **those who do** His commandments, that they may **have the right to the tree of life** [**Reward #69**], **may enter through the gates into the city** [**Reward #70**]. (Rev. 22:12–14)

Each of the above rewards **came after** someone spent time and/or money helping someone else. I hope you find it as interesting as I have that the last reward listed in the New Testament is that you may enter through the gates into the city. Any Christian reader who has taken the time to get this far will probably never hear Jesus say, "Depart. I knew you not." You would not have taken the time to finish reading this unless you know the loving, forgiving God we serve and trust and that there is still hope for us. **The Scriptures repeatedly remind us to never give up**. May we all trust Him with our time and money so that we can hear, "Well done, good and faithful servant!"

List of Rewards

#1 that you may be sons of your Father in heaven
#2 you shall be perfect
#3 your Father Himself will reward you openly
#4 protection for your heart
#5 food, drink, and clothing will be added
#6 enter the kingdom of heaven
#7 considered a wise man
#8 founded on the rock
#9 receive healing
#10 have demons cast out
#11 disease is cured
#12 household considered worthy
#13 peace comes upon your household
#14 be considered worthy of Jesus
#15 find your life
#16 receive God
#17 receive a prophet's reward
#18 receive a righteous man's reward
#19 rest for your soul
#20 receive return for your investment in Him
#21 have treasure in heaven
#22 inherit eternal life
#23 be called a good and faithful servant
#24 enter into the joy of the Lord
#25 have abundance
#26 you are blessed of God
#27 serving God
#28 have a memorial
#29 all things are clean to you
#30 receive the key of knowledge
#31 give God pleasure
#32 you shall be repaid
#33 receive true riches
#34 receive your own

#35 salvation for your household
#36 be raised from the dead
#37 help many believe in the Lord
#38 receive instruction from a holy angel
#39 remembered in the sight of God
#40 have the Holy Spirit fall on those around you
#41 bigger blessing
#42 receive the grace of God
#43 abundance of joy
#44 have an advantage
#45 sufficiency for all things
#46 increase fruits of your righteousness
#47 many thanksgivings to God
#48 others pray for you
#49 have exceeding grace of God
#50 receive the prize of the upward call of God
#51 not be unfruitful
#52 God is well pleased
#53 blessed in what he does
#54 your faith made perfect
#55 be called the friend of God
#56 be justified by works
#57 know love
#58 know you are of the truth
#59 assure your heart before God
#60 have confidence toward God
#61 whatever we ask, we receive from God
#62 we abide in God
#63 God abides in us
#64. give God no greater joy
#65 give witness of your love before the church
#66 you do well
#67 you are of God
#68 God rewards you
#69 have right to the tree of life
#70 enter through the gates into the city

70 PROPHECIES "WAS NEEDED"

The first 11 were written down by Moses more than 1300 years before the birth of Christ. At least 42 generations before His birth. They are recorded in the Torah which is also the first five books of the Old Testament. The remaining prophecies were given at least 500 years before His birth. Based on this recorded evidence, there is no way that Jesus is not "The Son of God". The risen last blood sacrifice for our sin's. To help see time involved it would be like someone giving prophecy in the year 700 AD with others giving more prophecy, about the same person or event, over seventy different ones, that stopped in year 1500 AD and all were fulfilled in year 2000 AD.

Genesis 3:14–15: "So the Lord God said to the serpent: 'Because you have done this, you are cursed more than all cattle and more than every beast of the field; On your belly you shall go and you shall eat dust All the days of your life. And I will put enmity between you and the woman and between your seed and her Seed; He shall bruise your head and you shall bruise His heel.'"

Galatians 4:4: "But when the fullness of the time had come, God sent forth His Son, born of a woman, born under the law."

Hebrews 2:14: "Inasmuch then as the children have partaken of flesh and blood, He Himself likewise shared in the same, that through death He might destroy him who had the power of death, that is, the devil."

First John 3:8: "He who sins is of the devil, for the devil has sinned from the beginning. For this purpose the Son of God was manifested, that He might destroy the works of the devil."

Genesis 12:3: "I will bless those who bless you, And I will curse him who curses you; And in you all the families of the earth shall be blessed."

Genesis 18:17–18: "And the Lord said, 'Shall I hide from Abraham what I am doing, since Abraham shall surely become a great and mighty nation, and all the nations of the earth shall be blessed in him?'"

Genesis 22:18: "In your seed all the nations of the earth shall be blessed, because you have obeyed My voice."

Genesis 26:2–4: "Then the Lord appeared to him and said: 'Do not go down to Egypt; live in the land of which I shall tell you. Dwell in this land, and I will be with you and bless you; for to you and your descendants I give all these lands, and I will perform the oath which I swore to Abraham your father. And I will make your descendants multiply as the stars of heaven; I will give to your descendants all these lands; and in your seed all the nations of the earth shall be blessed.'"

Acts 3:25–26: "You are sons of the prophets, and of the covenant which God made with our fathers, saying to Abraham, 'And in your seed all the families of the earth shall be blessed.' To you first, God, having raised up His Servant Jesus, sent Him to bless you, in turning away every one of you from your iniquities."

Genesis 17:7–8: "And I will establish My covenant between Me and you and your descendants after you in their generations, for an everlasting covenant, to be God to you and your descendants after you. Also I give to you and your descendants after you the land in which you are a stranger, all the land of Canaan, as an everlasting possession; and I will be their God."

Genesis 21:12: "But God said to Abraham, 'Do not let it be displeasing in your sight because of the lad or because of your bondwoman. Whatever Sarah has said to you, listen to her voice; for in Isaac your seed shall be called.'"

Galatians 3:16: "Now to Abraham and his Seed were the promises made. He does not say, 'And to seeds,' as of many, but as of one, 'And to your Seed,' who is Christ."

Hebrews 2:16: "For indeed He does not give aid to angels, but He does give aid to the seed of Abraham."

Genesis 17:19: "Then God said: 'No, Sarah your wife shall bear you a son, and you shall call his name Isaac; I will establish My covenant with him for an everlasting covenant, and with his descendants after him.'"

Genesis 21:12: "But God said to Abraham, 'Do not let it be displeasing in your sight because of the lad or because of your bondwoman. Whatever Sarah has said to you, listen to her voice; for in Isaac your seed shall be called.'"

Matthew 1:1–2: "The book of the genealogy of Jesus Christ, the Son of David, the Son of Abraham: Abraham begot Isaac, Isaac begot Jacob, and Jacob begot Judah and his brothers."

Romans 9:7: "Nor are they all children because they are the seed of Abraham; but, 'In Isaac your seed shall be called.'"

Hebrews 11:17–19: "By faith Abraham, when he was tested, offered up Isaac, and he who had received the promises offered up his only begotten son, of whom it was said, 'In Isaac your seed shall be called,' concluding that God was able to raise him up, even from the dead, from which he also received him in a figurative sense."

Genesis 49:8–10: "Judah, you are he whom your brothers shall praise; Your hand shall be on the neck of your enemies; Your father's children shall bow down before you. Judah is a lion's whelp; From the prey, my son, you have gone up. He bows down, he lies down as a lion; And as a lion, who shall rouse him? The scepter shall not depart from Judah, nor a lawgiver from between his feet, Until Shiloh comes And to Him shall be the obedience of the people."

Matthew 1:1–3: "The book of the genealogy of Jesus Christ, the Son of David, the Son of Abraham: Abraham begot Isaac, Isaac begot Jacob, and Jacob begot Judah and his brothers. Judah begot Perez and Zerah by Tamar, Perez begot Hezron, and Hezron begot Ram."

Hebrews 7:14: "For it is evident that our Lord arose from Judah, of which tribe Moses spoke nothing concerning priesthood."

Revelation 5:5: "But one of the elders said to me, 'Do not weep. Behold, the Lion of the tribe of Judah, the Root of David, has prevailed to open the scroll and to loose its seven seals.'"

Exodus 12:46: "In one house it shall be eaten; you shall not carry any of the flesh outside the house, nor shall you break one of its bones."

John 19:31–36: "Therefore, because it was the Preparation Day, that the bodies should not remain on the cross on the Sabbath (for that Sabbath was a high day), the Jews asked Pilate that their legs might be broken, and that they might be taken away. Then the soldiers came and broke the legs of the first and of the other who was crucified with Him. But when they came to Jesus and saw that He was already dead, they did not break His legs. But one of the soldiers pierced His side with a spear, and immediately blood and water came out. And he who has seen has testified, and his testimony is true; and he knows that he is telling the truth, so that you may believe. For these things were done that the Scripture should be fulfilled, 'Not one of His bones shall be broken.'"

Exodus 13:2: "'Consecrate to Me all the firstborn, whatever opens the womb among the children of Israel, both of man and beast; it is Mine."

Numbers 3:13: "Because all the firstborn are Mine. On the day that I struck all the firstborn in the land of Egypt, I sanctified to Myself all the firstborn in Israel, both man and beast. They shall be Mine: I am the Lord."

Numbers 8:17: "For all the firstborn among the children of Israel are Mine, both man and beast; on the day that I struck all the firstborn in the land of Egypt I sanctified them to Myself."

Luke 2:7: "And she brought forth her firstborn Son, and wrapped Him in swaddling cloths, and laid Him in a manger, because there was no room for them in the inn."

Numbers 9:12: "They shall leave none of it until morning, nor break one of its bones. According to all the ordinances of the Passover they shall keep it."

Deuteronomy 21:23: "His body shall not remain overnight on the tree, but you shall surely bury him that day, so that you do not defile the land which the Lord your God is giving you as an inheritance; for he who is hanged is accursed of God."

Galatians 3:134: "Christ has redeemed us from the curse of the law, having become a curse for us (for it is written, 'Cursed is everyone who hangs on a tree')."

John 19:31–36: "Therefore, because it was the Preparation Day, that the bodies should not remain on the cross on the Sabbath (for that Sabbath was a high day), the Jews asked Pilate that their legs might be broken, and that they might be taken away. Then the soldiers came and broke the legs of the first and of the other who was crucified with Him. But when they came to Jesus and saw that He was already dead, they did not break His legs. But one of the soldiers pierced His side with a spear, and immediately blood and water came out. And he who has seen has testified, and his testimony is true; and he knows that he is telling the truth, so that you may believe. For these things were done that the Scripture should be fulfilled, 'Not one of His bones shall be broken.'"

Numbers 24:17–19: "'I see Him, but not now; I behold Him, but not near; A Star shall come out of Jacob; A Scepter shall rise out of Israel and batter the brow of Moab and destroy all the sons of tumult. And Edom shall be a possession; Seir also, his enemies, shall be a possession, while Israel does valiantly. Out of Jacob One shall have dominion and destroy the remains of the city.'"

Matthew 1:2: "Abraham begot Isaac, Isaac begot Jacob, and Jacob begot Judah and his brothers."

Luke 1:33: "And He will reign over the house of Jacob forever, and of His kingdom there will be no end."

Deuteronomy 18:15: "'The Lord your God will raise up for you a Prophet like me from your midst, from your brethren. Him you shall hear.'"

Deuteronomy 18:18–19: "I will raise up for them a Prophet like you from among their brethren, and will put My words in His mouth, and He shall speak to them all that I command Him. And it shall be that whoever will not hear My words, which He speaks in My name, I will require it of him."

Matthew 21:11: "So the multitudes said, 'This is Jesus, the prophet from Nazareth of Galilee.'"

Luke 7:16: "Then fear came upon all, and they glorified God, saying, 'A great prophet has risen up among us'; and, 'God has visited His people.'"

John 6:14: "Then those men, when they had seen the sign that Jesus did, said, 'This is truly the Prophet who is to come into the world.'"

John 7:40 "Therefore many from the crowd, when they heard this saying, said, 'Truly this is the Prophet.'"

Acts 3:18–22: "But those things which God foretold by the mouth of all His prophets, that the Christ would suffer, He has thus fulfilled. Repent therefore and be converted, that your sins may be blotted out, so that times of refreshing may come from the presence of the Lord, and that He may send Jesus Christ, who was preached to you before, whom heaven must receive until the times of restoration of all things, which God has spoken by the mouth of all His holy prophets since the world began. For Moses truly said to the fathers, 'The Lord your God will raise up for you a Prophet like me from your brethren. Him you shall hear in all things, whatever He says to you.'"

2 Sam 7:12–13: "'When your days are fulfilled and you rest with your fathers, I will set up your seed after you, who will come from your body, and I will establish his kingdom. He shall build a house for My name, and I will establish the throne of his kingdom forever.'"

Matthew 1:1: "The book of the genealogy of Jesus Christ, the Son of David, the Son of Abraham."

Psalm 2:1–2: "Why do the nations rage, And the people plot a vain thing? The kings of the earth set themselves, And the rulers take counsel together, Against the Lord and against His Anointed."

Matthew 12:14: "Then the Pharisees went out and plotted against Him, how they might destroy Him."

Matthew 26:3–4: "Then the chief priests, the scribes, and the elders of the people assembled at the palace of the high priest, who was called Caiaphas, and plotted to take Jesus by trickery and kill Him."

Matthew 26:47: "And while He was still speaking, behold, Judas, one of the twelve, with a great multitude with swords and clubs, came from the chief priests and elders of the people."

Psalm 22:15–16: "My strength is dried up like a potsherd, And My tongue clings to My jaws; You have brought Me to the dust of death. For dogs have surrounded Me; The congregation of the wicked has enclosed Me. They pierced My hands and My feet."

John 20:25–29: "The other disciples therefore said to him, 'we have seen the Lord'. So he said to them, 'Unless I see in His hands the print of the nails, and put my finger into the print of the nails, and put my hand into His side, I will not believe.' And after eight days His disciples were again inside, and Thomas with them. Jesus came, the doors being shut, and stood in the midst, and said, 'Peace to you!' Then He said to Thomas, 'Reach your finger here, and look at My hands; and reach your hand here and put it into My side. Do not be unbelieving but believing.' And Thomas answered and said to Him, 'My Lord and my God!' Jesus said to him, 'Thomas, because you have seen Me, you have believed. Blessed are those who have not seen and yet have believed.'"

Psalm 22:18: "They divide My garments among them, And for My clothing they cast lots."

John 19:23–24: "Then the soldiers, when they had crucified Jesus, took His garments and made four parts, to each soldier a part and also the tunic. Now the tunic was without seam, woven from the top in one piece. They said therefore among themselves, 'Let us not tear it, but cast lots for it, whose it shall be,' that the Scripture might be fulfilled which says 'They divided My garments among them, And for My clothing they cast lots.' Therefore the soldiers did these things."

Psalm 27:12: "Do not deliver me to the will of my adversaries; For false witnesses have risen against me and such as breathe out violence."

Psalm 35:11: "Fierce witnesses rise up."

Matthew 26:60: "But found none. Even though many false witnesses came forward, they found none. But at last two false witnesses came forward."

Mark 14:55–61: "Now the chief priests and all the council sought testimony against Jesus to put Him to death but found none. For many bore false witness against Him, but their testimonies did not agree. Then some rose up and bore false witness against Him, saying, 'We heard Him say, "I will destroy this temple made with hands, and within three days I will build another made without hands."' But not even then did their testimony agree. And the high priest stood up in the midst and asked Jesus, saying, 'Do You answer nothing? What is it these men testify against You?' But He kept silent and answered nothing. Again the high priest asked Him, saying to Him, 'Are You the Christ, the Son of the Blessed?'"

Matthew 26:60–61: "But found none. Even though many false witnesses came forward, they found none. But at last two false witnesses came forward."

Mark 14:55–59: "Now the chief priests and all the council sought testimony against Jesus to put Him to death, but found none. For many bore false witness against Him, but their testimonies did not agree. Then some rose up and bore false witness against Him, saying, 'We heard Him say, "I will destroy this temple made with hands, and within three days I will build another made without hands."' But not even then did their testimony agree."

Psalm 35:19: "Let them not rejoice over me who are wrongfully my enemies; Nor let them wink with the eye who hate me without a cause."

John 15:24–25: "If I had not done among them the works which no one else did, they would have no sin; but now they have seen and also hated both Me and My Father. But this happened that the word might be fulfilled which is written in their law, 'They hated Me without a cause.'"

Psalm 40:7–8: "Then I said, 'Behold, I come; In the scroll of the book it is written of me. I delight to do Your will, O my God,
And Your law is within my heart.'"

Matthew 26:39: "He went a little farther and fell on His face, and prayed, saying, 'O My Father, if it is possible, let this cup pass from Me; nevertheless, not as I will, but as You will.'"

Hebrews 10:5–9: "Therefore, when He came into the world, He said: 'Sacrifice and offering You did not desire, but a body You have prepared for Me. In burnt offerings and sacrifices for sin You had no pleasure. Then I said, "Behold, I have come—In the volume of the book it is written of Me—To do Your will, O God."' Previously saying, 'Sacrifice and offering, burnt offerings, and offerings for sin You did not desire, nor had pleasure in them (which are offered according to the law),' then He said, 'Behold, I have come to do Your will, O God.' He takes away the first that He may establish the second."

Psalm 45:6–7: "Your throne, O God, is forever and ever; A scepter of righteousness is the scepter of Your kingdom. You love righteousness and hate wickedness; Therefore God, Your God, has anointed You With the oil of gladness more than Your companions."

Hebrews 1:8–9: "But to the Son He says: 'Your throne, O God, is forever and ever; A scepter of righteousness is the scepter of Your kingdom. You have loved righteousness and hated lawlessness; Therefore God, Your God, has anointed You With the oil of gladness more than Your companions.'"

Psalm 69:8–9: "I have become a stranger to my brothers, and an alien to my mother's children; Because zeal for Your house has eaten me up, And the reproaches of those who reproach You have fallen on me."

John 7:3–5: "His brothers therefore said to Him, 'Depart from here and go into Judea, that Your disciples also may see the works that You are doing. For no one does anything in secret while he himself seeks to be known openly. If You do these things, show Yourself to the world.' For even His brothers did not believe in Him."

Psalm 69:9: "Because zeal for Your house has eaten me up, And the reproaches of those who reproach You have fallen on me."
John 2:17: "Then His disciples remembered that it was written, 'Zeal for Your house has eaten Me up.'"

Psalm 69:20–22: "Reproach has broken my heart and I am full of heaviness; I looked for someone to take pity, but there was none; And for comforters, but I found none. They also gave me gall for my food and for my thirst they gave me vinegar to drink. Let their table become a snare before them, And their well-being a trap."
Matthew 27:34: "They gave Him sour wine mingled with gall to drink. But when He had tasted it, He would not drink."

Psalm 72:10–11: "The kings of Tarshish and of the isles Will bring presents; The kings of Sheba and Seba Will offer gifts. Yes, all kings shall fall down before Him; All nations shall serve Him."
Matthew 2:1–11: "Now after Jesus was born in Bethlehem of Judea in the days of Herod the king, behold, wise men from the East came to Jerusalem, saying, 'Where is He who has been born King of the Jews? For we have seen His star in the East and have come to worship Him.' When Herod the king heard this, he was troubled, and all Jerusalem with him. And when he had gathered all the chief priests and scribes of the people together, he inquired of them where the Christ was to be born. So they said to him, 'In Bethlehem of Judea, for thus it is written by the prophet: "But you, Bethlehem, in the land of Judah, Are not the least among the rulers of Judah; For out of you shall come a Ruler Who will shepherd My people Israel."' Then Herod, when he had secretly called the wise men, determined from them what time the star appeared. And he sent them to Bethlehem and said, 'Go and search carefully for the young Child, and when

you have found Him, bring back word to me, that I may come and worship Him also.' When they heard the king, they departed; and behold, the star which they had seen in the East went before them, till it came and stood over where the young Child was. When they saw the star, they rejoiced with exceedingly great joy. And when they had come into the house, they saw the young Child with Mary His mother, and fell down and worshiped Him. And when they had opened their treasures, they presented gifts to Him: gold, frankincense, and myrrh."

Psalm 72:12–14: "For He will deliver the needy when he cries, the poor also, and him who has no helper. He will spare the poor and needy and will save the souls of the needy. He will redeem their life from oppression and violence; And precious shall be their blood in His sight."

Luke 7:22: "Jesus answered and said to them, 'Go and tell John the things you have seen and heard: that the blind see, the lame walk, the lepers are cleansed, the deaf hear, the dead are raised, the poor have the gospel preached to them.'"

Psalm 78:2: "I will open my mouth in a parable; I will utter dark sayings of old."

Matthew 13:10–16: "And the disciples came and said to Him, 'Why do You speak to them in parables?' He answered and said to them, 'Because it has been given to you to know the mysteries of the kingdom of heaven, but to them it has not been given. For whoever has, to him more will be given, and he will have abundance; but whoever does not have, even what he has will be taken away from him. Therefore I speak to them in parables, because seeing they do not see, and hearing they do not hear, nor do they understand. And in them the prophecy of Isaiah is fulfilled, which says: "Hearing you will hear and shall not understand, And seeing you will see and not perceive; For the hearts of this people have grown dull. Their ears are hard of hearing, and their eyes they have closed, Lest they should see with their eyes and hear with their ears, Lest they should understand with their hearts and turn, So that I should heal them." But blessed are your eyes for they see, and your ears for they hear.'"

Psalm 109:4: "In return for my love they are my accusers, But I give myself to prayer."

Matthew 5:44: "But I say to you, love your enemies, bless those who curse you, do good to those who hate you, and pray for those who spitefully use you and persecute you."

Luke 23:34: "Then Jesus said, 'Father, forgive them, for they do not know what they do.'"

Psalm 110:4: "The Lord has sworn and will not relent, 'You are a priest forever According to the order of Melchizedek.'"

Hebrews 5:1–6: "For every high priest taken from among men is appointed for men in things pertaining to God, that he may offer both gifts and sacrifices for sins. He can have compassion on those who are ignorant and going astray, since he himself is also subject to weakness. Because of this he is required as for the people, so also for himself, to offer sacrifices for sins. And no man takes this honor to himself, but he who is called by God, just as Aaron was. A Priest Forever So also Christ did not glorify Himself to become High Priest, but it was He who said to Him: 'You are My Son, Today I have begotten You.' As He also says in another place: 'You are a priest forever According to the order of Melchizedek.'"

Hebrews 6:20: "Where the forerunner has entered for us, even Jesus, having become High Priest forever according to the order of Melchizedek."

Hebrews 7:15–17: "And it is yet far more evident if, in the likeness of Melchizedek, there arises another priest who has come, not according to the law of a fleshly commandment, but according to the power of an endless life. For He testifies: '"You are a priest forever According to the order of Melchizedek."'"

Psalm 118:22–23: "The stone which the builders rejected Has become the chief cornerstone. This was the Lord's doing;
It is marvelous in our eyes."

Matthew 21:42: "Jesus said to them, 'Have you never read in the Scriptures: "The stone which the builders rejected Has become the chief cornerstone. This was the Lord's doing and it is marvelous in our eyes"?'"

Isaiah 6:9–10: "And He said, 'Go, and tell this people: "Keep on hearing, but do not understand; Keep on seeing, but do not perceive.

Make the heart of this people dull, and their ears heavy, and shut their eyes; Lest they see with their eyes, and hear with their ears, and understand with their heart, and return and be healed."'"

Matthew 13:13–15: "Therefore I speak to them in parables, because seeing they do not see, and hearing they do not hear, nor do they understand. And in them the prophecy of Isaiah is fulfilled, which says: 'Hearing you will hear and shall not understand,

And seeing you will see and not perceive; For the hearts of this people have grown dull. Their ears are hard of hearing,

And their eyes they have closed, lest they should see with their eyes and hear with their ears, lest they should understand with their hearts and turn, so that I should heal them.'"

John 12:37–40: "But although He had done so many signs before them, they did not believe in Him, that the word of Isaiah the prophet might be fulfilled, which he spoke: 'Lord, who has believed our report? And to whom has the arm of the Lord been revealed?' Therefore they could not believe, because Isaiah said again: 'He has blinded their eyes and hardened their hearts, lest they should see with their eyes, lest they should understand with their hearts and turn, So that I should heal them.'"

Acts 28:24–27: "And some were persuaded by the things which were spoken, and some disbelieved. So when they did not agree among themselves, they departed after Paul had said one word: 'The Holy Spirit spoke rightly through Isaiah the prophet to our fathers, saying, "Go to this people and say: 'Hearing you will hear, and shall not understand; And seeing you will see, and not perceive; For the hearts of this people have grown dull. Their ears are hard of hearing and their eyes they have closed, lest they should see with their eyes and hear with their ears, Lest they should understand with their hearts and turn so that I should heal them.'""""

Isaiah 7:13–14: "Then he said, 'Hear now, O house of David! Is it a small thing for you to weary men, but will you weary my God also? Therefore the Lord Himself will give you a sign: Behold, the virgin shall conceive and bear a Son, and shall call His name Immanuel.'"

Matthew 1:18–23: "Now the birth of Jesus Christ was as follows: After His mother Mary was betrothed to Joseph, before they came together, she was found with child of the Holy Spirit. Then Joseph her husband, being a just man, and not wanting to make her a public example, was minded to put her away secretly. But while he thought about these things, behold, an angel of the Lord appeared to him in a dream, saying, 'Joseph, son of David, do not be afraid to take to you Mary your wife, for that which is conceived in her is of the Holy Spirit. And she will bring forth a Son, and you shall call His name Jesus, for He will save His people from their sins.' So all this was done that it might be fulfilled which was spoken by the Lord through the prophet, saying: 'Behold, the virgin shall be with child, and bear a Son, and they shall call His name Immanuel,' which is translated, 'God with us.'"

Luke 1:26–35: "Now in the sixth month the angel Gabriel was sent by God to a city of Galilee named Nazareth, to a virgin betrothed to a man whose name was Joseph, of the house of David. The virgin's name was Mary. And having come in, the angel said to her, 'Rejoice, highly favored one, the Lord is with you; blessed are you among women!' But when she saw him, she was troubled at his saying, and considered what manner of greeting this was. Then the angel said to her, 'Do not be afraid, Mary, for you have found favor with God. And behold, you will conceive in your womb and bring forth a Son and shall call His name Jesus. He will be great and will be called the Son of the Highest; and the Lord God will give Him the throne of His father David. And He will reign over the house of Jacob forever, and of His kingdom there will be no end.' Then Mary said to the angel, 'How can this be, since I do not know a man?' And the angel answered and said to her, 'The Holy Spirit will come upon you, and the power of the Highest will overshadow you; therefore, also, that Holy One who is to be born will be called the Son of God.'"

Isaiah 8:14: "He will be as a sanctuary, But a stone of stumbling and a rock of offense to both the houses of Israel, As a trap and a snare to the inhabitants of Jerusalem."

Romans 9:31–33: "But Israel, pursuing the law of righteousness, has not attained to the law of righteousness. Why? Because they did not seek it by faith, but as it were, by the works of the law. For they stumbled at that stumbling stone. As it is written: 'Behold, I lay in Zion a stumbling stone and rock of offense, and whoever believes on Him will not be put to shame.'"

First Peter 2:7–8: "Therefore, to you who believe, He is precious; but to those who are disobedient, 'The stone which the builders rejected Has become the chief cornerstone,' and 'A stone of stumbling and a rock of offense.' They stumble, being disobedient to the word, to which they also were appointed."

Isaiah 9:1–2: "Nevertheless the gloom will not be upon her who is distressed, as when at first, He lightly esteemed the land of Zebulun and the land of Naphtali, and afterward more heavily oppressed her, By the way of the sea, beyond the Jordan, In Galilee of the Gentiles. The people who walked in darkness Have seen a great light; Those who dwelt in the land of the shadow of death, upon them a light has shined."

Matthew 4:12–16: "Now when Jesus heard that John had been put in prison, He departed to Galilee. And leaving Nazareth, He came and dwelt in Capernaum, which is by the sea, in the regions of Zebulun and Naphtali, that it might be fulfilled which was spoken by Isaiah the prophet, saying: 'The land of Zebulun and the land of Naphtali, By the way of the sea, beyond the Jordan, Galilee of the Gentiles: The people who sat in darkness have seen a great light, And upon those who sat in the region and shadow of death Light has dawned.'"

Isaiah 9:6: "For unto us a Child is born, unto us a Son is given; And the government will be upon His shoulder. And His name will be called Wonderful, Counselor, Mighty God, Everlasting Father, Prince of Peace."

Isaiah 9:7: "Of the increase of His government and peace There will be no end, Upon the throne of David and over His kingdom, To order it and establish it with judgment and justice from that time forward, even forever. The zeal of the Lord of hosts will perform this."

Luke 2:11: "For there is born to you this day in the city of David a Savior, who is Christ the Lord."

Matthew 1:1: "The book of the genealogy of Jesus Christ, the Son of David, the Son of Abraham."

Luke 1:32: "He will be great and will be called the Son of the Highest; and the Lord God will give Him the throne of His father David."

Luke 2:11: "For there is born to you this day in the city of David a Savior, who is Christ the Lord."

Acts 13:22–23: "And when He had removed him, He raised up for them David as king, to whom also He gave testimony and said, 'I have found David the son of Jesse, a man after My own heart, who will do all My will.' From this man's seed, according to the promise, God raised up for Israel a Savior—Jesus."

Isaiah 11:1–2: "There shall come forth a Rod from the stem of Jesse And a Branch shall grow out of his roots. The Spirit of the Lord shall rest upon Him, The Spirit of wisdom and understanding, The Spirit of counsel and might, The Spirit of knowledge and of the fear of the Lord."

Matthew 1:6: "And Jesse begot David the king."

Acts 13:22–23: "And when He had removed him, He raised up for them David as king, to whom also He gave testimony and said, 'I have found David the son of Jesse, a man after My own heart, who will do all My will.' From this man's seed, according to the promise, God raised up for Israel a Savior—Jesus."

Isaiah 11:2: "The Spirit of the Lord shall rest upon Him, The Spirit of wisdom and understanding, The Spirit of counsel and might, The Spirit of knowledge and of the fear of the Lord."

Matthew 3:16: "When He had been baptized, Jesus came up immediately from the water; and behold, the heavens were opened to Him, and He saw the Spirit of God descending like a dove and alighting upon Him."

Mark 1:10: "And immediately, coming up from the water, He saw the heavens parting and the Spirit descending upon Him like a dove.

Luke 3:22: "And the Holy Spirit descended in bodily form like a dove upon Him, and a voice came from heaven which said, 'You are My beloved Son; in You I am well pleased.'"

Luke 4:18: "'The Spirit of the Lord is upon Me, Because He has anointed Me To preach the gospel to the poor; He has sent Me to heal the brokenhearted, to proclaim liberty to the captives and recovery of sight to the blind to set at liberty those who are oppressed.'"

John 1:32: "And John bore witness, saying, 'I saw the Spirit descending from heaven like a dove, and He remained upon Him.'"

John 3:34: "For He whom God has sent speaks the words of God, for God does not give the Spirit by measure."

Acts 10:38: "How God anointed Jesus of Nazareth with the Holy Spirit and with power, who went about doing good and healing all who were oppressed by the devil, for God was with Him."

Isaiah 29:18: "In that day the deaf shall hear the words of the book, And the eyes of the blind shall see out of obscurity and out of darkness."

Matthew 11:5: "The blind see and the lame walk; the lepers are cleansed and the deaf hear; the dead are raised up and the poor have the gospel preached to them."

John 9:39: "And Jesus said, 'For judgment I have come into this world, that those who do not see may see, and that those who see may be made blind.'"

Luke 7:19–22: "And John, calling two of his disciples to him, sent them to Jesus, saying, 'Are You the Coming One, or do we look for another?' When the men had come to Him, they said, 'John the Baptist has sent us to You, saying, "Are You the Coming One, or do we look for another?"' And that very hour He cured many of infirmities, afflictions, and evil spirits; and to many blind He gave sight. Jesus answered and said to them, 'Go and tell John the things you have seen and heard: that the blind see, the lame walk, the lepers are cleansed, the deaf hear, the dead are raised, the poor have the gospel preached to them.'"

Mark 7:37: "And they were astonished beyond measure, saying, 'He has done all things well. He makes both the deaf to hear and the mute to speak.'"

Isaiah 35:4–6: "Say to those who are fearful-hearted, 'Be strong, do not fear! Behold, your God will come with vengeance, With the recompense of God; He will come and save you.' Then the eyes of the blind shall be opened, And the ears of the deaf shall be unstopped. Then the lame shall leap like a deer and the tongue of the dumb sing. For waters shall burst forth in the wilderness,
And streams in the desert."

Matthew 9:30: "And their eyes were opened. And Jesus sternly warned them, saying, 'See that no one knows it.'"

Matthew 11:4–6: "Jesus answered and said to them, 'Go and tell John the things which you hear and see: The blind see and the lame walk; the lepers are cleansed and the deaf hear; the dead are raised up and the poor have the gospel preached to them. And blessed is he who is not offended because of Me.'"

Matthew 12:22: "Then one was brought to Him who was demon-possessed, blind and mute; and He healed him, so that the blind and mute man both spoke and saw."

Matthew 20:34: "So Jesus had compassion and touched their eyes. And immediately their eyes received sight, and they followed Him."

Matthew 21:14: "Then the blind and the lame came to Him in the temple, and He healed them."

Mark 7:32–35: "Then they brought to Him one who was deaf and had an impediment in his speech, and they begged Him to put

His hand on him. And He took him aside from the multitude, and put His fingers in his ears, and He spat and touched his tongue. Then, looking up to heaven, He sighed, and said to him, 'Ephphatha,' that is, 'Be opened.' Immediately his ears were opened, and the impediment of his tongue was loosed, and he spoke plainly."

John 9:1–7: "Now as Jesus passed by, He saw a man who was blind from birth. And His disciples asked Him, saying, 'Rabbi, who sinned, this man or his parents, that he was born blind?' Jesus answered, 'Neither this man nor his parents sinned, but that the works of God should be revealed in him. I must work the works of Him who sent Me while it is day; the night is coming when no one can work. As long as I am in the world, I am the light of the world.' When He had said these things, He spat on the ground and made clay with the saliva; and He anointed the eyes of the blind man with the clay. And He said to him, 'Go, wash in the pool of Siloam (which is translated, Sent).' So he went and washed, and came back seeing."

John 11:47: "Then the chief priests and the Pharisees gathered a council and said, 'What shall we do? For this Man works many signs.'"

Isaiah 40:3–4: "The voice of one crying in the wilderness: 'Prepare the way of the Lord; Make straight in the desert A highway for our God. Every valley shall be exalted and every mountain and hill brought low; The crooked places shall be made straight And the rough places smooth."

Matthew 3:3: "For this is he who was spoken of by the prophet Isaiah, saying: 'The voice of one crying in the wilderness: "Prepare the way of the Lord; Make His paths straight."'"

Mark 1:3: "'The voice of one crying in the wilderness: "Prepare the way of the Lord; Make His paths straight."'"

Luke 3:3–5: "And he went into all the region around the Jordan, preaching a baptism of repentance for the remission of sins, as it is written in the book of the words of Isaiah the prophet, saying: 'The voice of one crying in the wilderness: "Prepare the way of the Lord; Make His paths straight. Every valley shall be filled and every mountain and hill brought low; The crooked places shall be made straight And the rough ways smooth.""'"

Luke 3:3–5: "And he went into all the region around the Jordan, preaching a baptism of repentance for the remission of sins, as it is written in the book of the words of Isaiah the prophet, saying: 'The voice of one crying in the wilderness: "Prepare the way of the Lord; Make His paths straight. Every valley shall be filled and every mountain and hill brought low; The crooked places shall be made straight And the rough ways smooth.""'"

John 1:23: "He said: 'I am "The voice of one crying in the wilderness: 'Make straight the way of the Lord,'" as the prophet Isaiah said.'"

Isaiah 40:10–11: "Behold, the Lord God shall come with a strong hand, And His arm shall rule for Him; Behold, His reward is with Him, And His work before Him. He will feed His flock like a shepherd; He will gather the lambs with His arm, and carry them in His bosom, And gently lead those who are with young."

John 10:11: "'I am the good shepherd. The good shepherd gives His life for the sheep.'"

Hebrews 13:20: "Now may the God of peace who brought up our Lord Jesus from the dead, that great Shepherd of the sheep, through the blood of the everlasting covenant."

First Peter 2:25: "For you were like sheep going astray but have now returned to the Shepherd and Overseer of your souls."

Isaiah 42:1–4: "'Behold! My Servant whom I uphold, My Elect One in whom My soul delights! I have put My Spirit upon Him; He will bring forth justice to the Gentiles. He will not cry out, nor raise His voice, nor cause His voice to be heard in the street. A bruised reed He will not break and smoking flax He will not quench; He will bring forth justice for truth. He will not fail nor be discouraged, Till He has established justice in the earth; And the coastlands shall wait for His law.'"

Matthew 12:16–21: "Yet He warned them not to make Him known, that it might be fulfilled which was spoken by Isaiah the prophet, saying: 'Behold! My Servant whom I have chosen, My Beloved in whom My soul is well pleased! I will put My Spirit upon Him, And He will declare justice to the Gentiles. He will not quarrel nor cry out, Nor will anyone hear His voice in the streets. A bruised reed He will not break and smoking flax He will not quench, Till He sends forth justice to victory; And in His name Gentiles will trust.'"

Isaiah 42:6: "'I, the Lord, have called You in righteousness and will hold Your hand; I will keep You and give You as a covenant to the people, As a light to the Gentiles.'"

Luke 2:25–32: "And behold, there was a man in Jerusalem whose name was Simeon, and this man was just and devout, waiting for the Consolation of Israel, and the Holy Spirit was upon him. And it had been revealed to him by the Holy Spirit that he would not see death before he had seen the Lord's Christ. So he came by the Spirit into the temple. And when the parents brought in the Child Jesus, to do for Him according to the custom of the law, he took Him up in his arms and blessed God and said: 'Lord, now You are letting Your servant depart in peace, According to Your word; For my eyes have seen Your salvation Which You have prepared before the face of all peoples, A light to bring revelation to the Gentiles, And the glory of Your people Israel.'"

Acts 26:23: "'That the Christ would suffer, that He would be the first to rise from the dead and would proclaim light to the Jewish people and to the Gentiles.'"

Isaiah 50:6: "I gave My back to those who struck Me, And My cheeks to those who plucked out the beard; I did not hide My face from shame and spitting."

Matthew 26:67–68: "Then they spat in His face and beat Him; and others struck Him with the palms of their hands, saying, 'Prophesy to us, Christ! Who is the one who struck You?'"

Matthew 27:26–29: "Then he released Barabbas to them; and when he had scourged Jesus, he delivered Him to be crucified. Then the soldiers of the governor took Jesus into the Praetorium and gathered the whole garrison around Him. And they stripped Him and put a scarlet robe on Him. When they had twisted a crown of thorns, they put it on His head, and a reed in His right hand. And they bowed the knee before Him and mocked Him, saying, 'Hail, King of the Jews!'"

Mark 14:65: "Then some began to spit on Him, and to blindfold Him, and to beat Him, and to say to Him, 'Prophesy!' And the officers struck Him with the palms of their hands."

Mark 15:15–19: "So Pilate, wanting to gratify the crowd, released Barabbas to them; and he delivered Jesus, after he had scourged Him, to be crucified. The Soldiers Mock Jesus Then the soldiers led Him away into the hall called Praetorium, and they called together the whole garrison. And they clothed Him with purple; and they twisted a crown of thorns, put it on His head, and began to salute Him, 'Hail, King of the Jews!' Then they struck Him on the head with a reed and spat on Him; and bowing the knee, they worshiped Him."

Luke 22:63–65: "Now the men who held Jesus mocked Him and beat Him. And having blindfolded Him, they struck Him on the face and asked Him, saying, 'Prophesy! Who is the one who struck You?' And many other things they blasphemously spoke against Him."

John 19:1: "So then Pilate took Jesus and scourged Him."

Isaiah 55:4–5: "'Indeed I have given him as a witness to the people, A leader and commander for the people. Surely you shall call a nation you do not know, and nations who do not know you shall run to you, Because of the Lord your God, And the Holy One of Israel; For He has glorified you.'"

Romans 9:23–26: "And that He might make known the riches of His glory on the vessels of mercy, which He had prepared beforehand for glory, even us whom He called, not of the Jews only, but also of the Gentiles? As He says also in Hosea: 'I will call them My people, who were not My people, And her beloved, who was not beloved.' 'And it shall come to pass in the place where it was said to them, "You are not My people," There they shall be called sons of the living God.'"

Isaiah 59:20: "'The Redeemer will come to Zion and to those who turn from transgression in Jacob,' Says the Lord."

Romans 11:26–27: "And so all Israel will be saved, as it is written: 'The Deliverer will come out of Zion, And He will turn away ungodliness from Jacob; For this is My covenant with them, When I take away their sins.'"

Isaiah 61:1–2: "'The Spirit of the Lord God is upon Me, Because the Lord has anointed Me To preach good tidings to the poor; He has sent Me to heal the brokenhearted to proclaim liberty to the captives, And the opening of the prison to those who are bound;

To proclaim the acceptable year of the Lord, And the day of vengeance of our God; To comfort all who mourn.'"

Luke 4:16–21: "So He came to Nazareth, where He had been brought up. And as His custom was, He went into the synagogue on the Sabbath day, and stood up to read. And He was handed the book of the prophet Isaiah. And when He had opened the book, He found the place where it was written: 'The Spirit of the Lord is upon Me, Because He has anointed Me To preach the gospel to the poor; He has sent Me to heal the brokenhearted, To proclaim liberty to the captives And recovery of sight to the blind, To set at liberty those who are oppressed; To proclaim the acceptable year of the Lord.' Then He closed the book, and gave it back to the attendant and sat down. And the eyes of all who were in the synagogue were fixed on Him. And He began to say to them, 'Today this Scripture is fulfilled in your hearing.'"

Acts 10:38: "How God anointed Jesus of Nazareth with the Holy Spirit and with power, who went about doing good and healing all who were oppressed by the devil, for God was with Him."

Jeremiah 31:15: "Thus says the Lord: 'A voice was heard in Ramah, Lamentation and bitter weeping, Rachel weeping for her children,

Refusing to be comforted for her children because they are no more.'"

Matthew 2:16: "Then Herod, when he saw that he was deceived by the wise men, was exceedingly angry; and he sent forth and put to death all the male children who were in Bethlehem and in all its districts, from two years old and under, according to the time which he had determined from the wise men."

Jeremiah 31:31–34: "'Behold, the days are coming,' says the Lord, 'when I will make a new covenant with the house of Israel and with the house of Judah—not according to the covenant that I made with their fathers in the day that I took them by the hand to lead them out of the land of Egypt, My covenant which they broke, though I was a husband to them,' says the Lord. 'But this is the covenant that I will make with the house of Israel after those days,' says the Lord: 'I will put My law in their minds, and write it on their hearts; and I will be their God, and they shall be My people. No more shall every man teach his neighbor, and every man his brother, saying, "Know the Lord," for they all shall know Me, from the least of them to the greatest of them,' says the Lord. 'For I will forgive their iniquity, and their sin I will remember no more.'"

Jeremiah 32:37–40: "Behold, I will gather them out of all countries where I have driven them in My anger, in My fury, and in great wrath; I will bring them back to this place, and I will cause them to dwell safely. They shall be My people, and I will be their God; then I will give them one heart and one way, that they may fear Me forever, for the good of them and their children after them. And I will make an everlasting covenant with them, that I will not turn away from doing them good; but I will put My fear in their hearts so that they will not depart from Me."

Luke 22:15–20: "Then He said to them, 'With fervent desire I have desired to eat this Passover with you before I suffer; for I say to you, I will no longer eat of it until it is fulfilled in the kingdom of God.' Then He took the cup, and gave thanks, and said, 'Take this and divide it among yourselves; for I say to you, I will not drink of the fruit of the vine until the kingdom of God comes.'

And He took bread, gave thanks and broke it, and gave it to them, saying, 'This is My body which is given for you; do this in remembrance of Me.' Likewise He also took the cup after supper, saying, 'This cup is the new covenant in My blood, which is shed for you.'"

Hebrews 10:15–20: "But the Holy Spirit also witnesses to us; for after He had said before, 'This is the covenant that I will make with them after those days, says the Lord: I will put My laws into their hearts, and in their minds I will write them,' then He adds, 'Their sins and their lawless deeds I will remember no more.' Now where there is remission of these, there is no longer an offering for sin. Therefore, brethren, having boldness to enter the Holiest by the blood of Jesus, by a new and living way which He consecrated for us, through the veil, that is, His flesh."

Hosea 2:23: "Then I will sow her for Myself in the earth, And I will have mercy on her who had not obtained mercy; Then I will say to those who were not My people, 'You are My people!' And they shall say, 'You are my God!'"

Romans 9:23–26: "And that He might make known the riches of His glory on the vessels of mercy, which He had prepared beforehand for glory, even us whom He called, not of the Jews only, but also of the Gentiles? As He says also in Hosea: 'I will call them My people, who were not My people, And her beloved, who was not beloved.' 'And it shall come to pass in the place where it was said to them, "You are not My people," There they shall be called sons of the living God.'"

Hosea 11:1: "'When Israel was a child, I loved him and out of Egypt I called My son.'"

Matthew 2:13–15: "Now when they had departed, behold, an angel of the Lord appeared to Joseph in a dream, saying, 'Arise, take the young Child and His mother, flee to Egypt, and stay there until I bring you word; for Herod will seek the young Child to destroy Him.' When he arose, he took the young Child and His mother by night and departed for Egypt, and was there until the death of Herod, that it might be fulfilled which was spoken by the Lord through the prophet, saying, 'Out of Egypt I called My Son.'"

Matthew 19:21: "Jesus said to him, 'If you want to be perfect, go, sell what you have and give to the poor, and you will have treasure in heaven; and come, follow Me.'"

Joel 2:28–32: "'And it shall come to pass afterward That I will pour out My Spirit on all flesh; Your sons and your daughters shall prophesy, Your old men shall dream dreams, Your young men shall see visions. And also on My menservants and on My maid servants I will pour out My Spirit in those days. "And I will show wonders in the heavens and in the earth: Blood and fire and pillars of smoke. The sun shall be turned into darkness, And the moon into blood, Before the coming of the great and awesome day of the Lord. And it shall come to pass That whoever calls on the name of the Lord Shall be saved. For in Mount Zion and in Jerusalem there shall be deliverance, As the Lord has said, Among the remnant whom the Lord calls."'"

Acts 2:16–23: "But this is what was spoken by the prophet Joel: 'And it shall come to pass in the last days, says God, That I will pour out of My Spirit on all flesh; Your sons and your daughters shall prophesy, your young men shall see visions, Your old men shall dream dreams. And on My menservants and on My maid servants I will pour out My Spirit in those days; And they shall prophesy. I will show wonders in heaven above And signs in the earth beneath: Blood and fire and vapor of smoke. The sun shall be turned into darkness, And the moon into blood before the coming of the great and awesome day of the Lord. And it shall come to pass That whoever calls on the name of the Lord Shall be saved.' 'Men of Israel, hear these words: Jesus of Nazareth, a Man attested by God to you by miracles, wonders, and signs which God did through Him in your midst, as you yourselves also know—Him, being delivered by the determined purpose and foreknowledge of God, you have taken by lawless hands, have crucified, and put to death.'"

Amos 9:11–12: "'On that day I will raise up the tabernacle of David, which has fallen down and repair its damages. I will raise up its ruins and rebuild it as in the days of old; That they may possess the remnant of Edom and all the Gentiles who are called by My name,' Says the Lord who does this thing."

Acts 15:16–18: "'After! this I will return and will rebuild the tabernacle of David, which has fallen down; I will rebuild its ruins, And I will set it up; So that the rest of mankind may seek the Lord, even all the Gentiles who are called by My name,' Says the Lord who does all these things. 'Known to God from eternity are all His works.'"

Micah 5:1: "Now gather yourself in troops, O daughter of troops; He has laid siege against us; They will strike the judge of Israel with a rod on the cheek."

Matthew 27:30: "Then they spat on Him and took the reed and struck Him on the head."

Micah 5:2–5: "'But you, Bethlehem Ephrathah, though you are little among the thousands of Judah yet out of you shall come forth to Me the One to be Ruler in Israel, whose goings forth are from of old, from everlasting.' Therefore He shall give them up,

Until the time that she who is in labor has given birth; Then the remnant of His brethren Shall return to the children of Israel.

And He shall stand and feed His flock in the strength of the Lord, In the majesty of the name of the Lord His God and they shall abide, for now He shall be great to the ends of the earth; And this One shall be peace. Judgment on Israel's Enemies When the Assyrian comes into our land and when he treads in our palaces, then we will raise against him Seven shepherds and eight princely men."

Matthew 2:1–6: "Now after Jesus was born in Bethlehem of Judea in the days of Herod the king, behold, wise men from the East came to Jerusalem, saying, 'Where is He who has been born King of the Jews? For we have seen His star in the East and have come to worship Him.' When Herod the king heard this, he was troubled, and all Jerusalem with him. And when he had gathered all the chief priests and scribes of the people together, he inquired of them where the Christ was to be born. So they said to him, 'In Bethlehem of Judea, for thus it is written by the prophet: "But you, Bethlehem, in the land of Judah are not the least among the rulers of Judah for out of you shall come a Ruler Who will shepherd My people Israel."'"

Zechariah 2:10–13: "'Sing and rejoice, O daughter of Zion! For behold, I am coming and I will dwell in your midst,' says the Lord. 'Many nations shall be joined to the Lord in that day, and they shall become My people. And I will dwell in your midst. Then you will know that the Lord of hosts has sent Me to you. And the Lord will take possession of Judah as His inheritance in the Holy Land and will again choose Jerusalem. Be silent, all flesh, before the Lord, for He is aroused from His holy habitation!'"

John 1:14: "And the Word became flesh and dwelt among us, and we beheld His glory, the glory as of the only begotten of the Father, full of grace and truth."

Revelation 21:3: "And I heard a loud voice from heaven saying, 'Behold, the tabernacle of God is with men, and He will dwell with them, and they shall be His people. God Himself will be with them and be their God.'"

Zechariah 9:9: "'Rejoice greatly, O daughter of Zion! Shout, O daughter of Jerusalem! Behold, your King is coming to you; He is just and having salvation, Lowly and riding on a donkey, A colt, the foal of a donkey.'"

Mark 11:1–10: "Now when they drew near Jerusalem, to Bethphage and Bethany, at the Mount of Olives, He sent two of His disciples; and He said to them, 'Go into the village opposite you; and as soon as you have entered it you will find a colt tied, on which no one has sat. Loose it and bring it. And if anyone says to you, "Why are you doing this?" say, "The Lord has need of it," and immediately he will send it here.' So they went their way, and found the colt tied by the door outside on the street, and they loosed it. But some of those who stood there said to them, 'What are you doing loosing the colt?' And they spoke to them just as Jesus had commanded. So they let them go. Then they brought the colt to Jesus and threw their clothes on it, and He sat on it. And many spread their clothes on the road, and others cut down leafy branches from the trees and spread them on the road. Then those who went before and those who followed cried out, saying: 'Hosanna! "Blessed is He who comes in the name of the Lord!" Blessed is the kingdom of our father David That comes in the name of the Lord! Hosanna in the highest!'"

Matthew 21:1–5: "Now when they drew near Jerusalem, and came to Bethphage, at the Mount of Olives, then Jesus sent two disciples, saying to them, 'Go into the village opposite you, and immediately you will find a donkey tied, and a colt with her. Loose them and bring them to Me. And if anyone says anything to you, you shall say, "The Lord has need of them," and immediately he will send them.' All this was done that it might be fulfilled which was spoken by the prophet, saying: 'Tell the daughter of Zion,

"Behold, your King is coming to you, Lowly, and sitting on a donkey, A colt, the foal of a donkey."'"

Luke 19:28–38: "When He had said this, He went on ahead, going up to Jerusalem. And it came to pass, when He drew near to Bethphage and Bethany, at the mountain called Olivet, that He sent two of His disciples, saying, 'Go into the village opposite you, where as you enter you will find a colt tied, on which no one has ever sat. Loose it and bring it here. And if anyone asks you, "Why are you loosing it?" thus you shall say to him, "Because the Lord has need of it."' So those who were sent went their way and found it just as He had said to them. But as they were loosing the colt, the owners of it said to them, 'Why are you loosing the colt?' And they said, 'The Lord has need of him.' Then they brought him to Jesus. And they threw their own clothes on the colt, and they set Jesus on him. And as He went, many spread their clothes on the road. Then, as He was now drawing near the descent of the Mount of Olives, the whole multitude of the disciples began to rejoice and praise God with a loud voice for all the mighty works they had seen, saying: '"Blessed is the King who comes in the name of the Lord!" Peace in heaven and glory in the highest!'"

John 12:14–15: "Then Jesus, when He had found a young donkey, sat on it; as it is written: 'Fear not, daughter of Zion; Behold, your King is coming, Sitting on a donkey's colt.'"

Malachi 4:5–6: "'Behold, I will send you Elijah the prophet Before the coming of the great and dreadful day of the Lord. And he will turn The hearts of the fathers to the children, And the hearts of the children to their fathers, Lest I come and strike the earth with a curse.'"

Matthew 11:13–14: "For all the prophets and the law prophesied until John. And if you are willing to receive it, he is Elijah who is to come."

Mark 9:11–13: "And they asked Him, saying, 'Why do the scribes say that Elijah must come first?' Then He answered and told them, 'Indeed, Elijah is coming first and restores all things. And how is it written concerning the Son of Man, that He must suffer many things and be treated with contempt? But I say to you that Elijah has also come, and they did to him whatever they wished, as it is written of him.'"

Luke 1:17: "'He will also go before Him in the spirit and power of Elijah, "to turn the hearts of the fathers to the children," and the disobedient to the wisdom of the just, to make ready a people prepared for the Lord.'"

Luke 7:27–28: "'This is he of whom it is written: "Behold, I send My messenger before Your face, Who will prepare Your way before You." For I say to you, among those born of women there is not a greater prophet than John the Baptist; but he who is least in the kingdom of God is greater than he.'"

List of 70 prophecies "was needed"

The first 11 were written down by Moses more than 1300 years before the birth of Christ. At least 42 generations before His birth. They are recorded in the Torah which is also the first five books of the Old Testament. The remaining prophecies were given at least 500 years before His birth. Based on this recorded evidence, there is no way that Jesus is not "The Son of God". The risen last blood sacrifice for our sin's. To help see time involved it would be like someone giving prophecy in the year 700 AD with others giving more prophecy, about the same Person or event, over seventy different ones, that stopped in year 1500 AD and all were fulfilled in year 2000 AD.

1. I will put empathy between
2. Will bruise Satan's head
3. all families and nations blessed through Abraham's seed

4. I will establish my covenant with Abraham
5. be from the seed of Isaac
6. being from the seed of Judah
7. have no broken bones
8. consecrated to God
9. not left overnight on the cross
10. be from the seed of Jacob
11. be a prophet
12. God will establish the throne of his kingdom
13. the rulers of King's counsel together against
14. pierce his hands and feet
15. soldiers divide garments
16. cast lots for his clothing
17. false witnesses coming against
18. hated without cause
19. do God's will
20. love righteousness
21. hate wickedness
22. stranger to his own brothers
23. zeal for God's house
24. given gall for food
25. did given vinegar to drink
26. King's bring presents and gifts
27. kings will worship him
28. He will deliver the needy
29. will speak in parables
30. give himself to prayer
31. a priest forever according to the order of Melchizedek
32. builders reject
33. become chief cornerstone
34. people will not hear and see
35. Virgin's firstborn is a son
36. His name Immanuel
37. He will be as a sanctuary
38. a stone of stumbling
39. a rock of offense

40. ministry in Zebulum and the land of Naphtali
41. government will rest on his shoulder
42. to order it and establish it with judgment and justice
43. be from the stem of Jesse
44. Spirit of the Lord shall rest upon
45. deaf shall hear
46. blind shall see
47. Will heal the lame
48. will heal tongue of the dumb
49. voice of one crying in the wilderness
50. is like a shepherd
51. God will delight him
52. be as a light to the Gentiles
53. will be whipped
54. Beard plucked
55. will be spit upon
56. as a witness to the people
57. will come to Zion
58. anointed preach
59. Rachel will reap for her children
60. will make a new covenant
61. I will be there God, they shall be my people
62. of his people
63. His name Israel
64. come out of Egypt
65. will pour out his Spirit
66. Jerusalem there shall be deliverance
67. who's going forth are from of old, from everlasting
68. whoever calls on the name of the Lord shall be saved
69. will dwell in our midst
70. Will send Elijah

CPSIA information can be obtained
at www.ICGtesting.com
Printed in the USA
FSHW010929140919
61939FS

9 781098 006754